The Body Eclectic

The

AN ANTHOLOGY OF POEMS

EDITED BY

Patrice Vecchione

HENRY HOLT AND COMPANY · NEW YORK

Henry Holt and Company, LLC
Publishers since 1866
115 West 18th Street
New York, New York 10011
www.henryholt.com

Henry Holt is a registered trademark of Henry Holt and Company, LLC
Compilation and introduction copyright © 2002 by Patrice Vecchione
All rights reserved.
Distributed in Canada by H. B. Fenn and Company Ltd.

Library of Congress Cataloging-in-Publication Data
The body eclectic : an anthology of poems / edited by Patrice Vecchione.
p.   cm.
Includes bibliographical references and indexes.
1. Body, human—Poetry. 2. Children's poetry. I. Vecchione, Patrice.
PN6110.B75 B54 2002   808.81'935—dc21   2001051900

ISBN 0-8050-6935-6
First Edition—2002
Printed in the United States of America on acid-free paper. ∞
1   3   5   7   9   10   8   6   4   2

To the body, its wisdom,
and the poetry you find there

Acknowledgments

Marion Silverbear was my right hand on this project. I'm grateful for her assistance and her friendship. Many thanks to Charlotte Raymond, and to Alyssa Raymond—poem finder. Thanks to my editor, Laura Godwin—for the title!—and for her enthusiastic support of this project, and to her editorial assistant, Kate Farrell, who was always there when I needed her. For research assistance, thanks to Selene Hausman. For help with the biographies, thanks to Janet Greenberg and Morton Marcus. The Monterey City Library offered essential support to me—their team of reference librarians is superb. I received help particularly from Victor H. Bausch, Doug Holtzman, and Steve Parker. And Bridget McConnell, interlibrary-loan diva, I thank her for finding what otherwise wouldn't have been found, and for her graciousness. Thanks to my husband, Michael Stark; he knows for what.

Contents

The
Body
Eclectic

Introduction

When I began the work of finding poems for this collection, I had the faulty idea that I'd have one poem for each thing the body is or does. Impossible! I found some poems about parts of our bodies that are usually visible: One of Natasha Trethewey's poems is about hair, and Jane Hirshfield looks closely at the hand. Marge Piercy even honors the often-neglected heel of the foot. There are also poems about body parts that are usually hidden: Keelyn T. Healy discovers her breasts; Lin Max celebrates the vagina; the penis is written about by Erin Belieu. I've included some poems that look at the body as a whole entity. All of the poems, I hope, explore the body without objectifying it.

What is your favorite part of your body? Do you celebrate it, show it off, or cover it up? Could you write about fat as poet Lyn Lifshin does? Do you know what it's like to have your body injured by the hands of another? Playwright Claire Braz-Valentine taught writing to kids in juvenile hall, and they produced a play I've excerpted here about the violence humans do to one another. William Stafford writes about scars and their beauty. And Lucy Grealy describes what it was like to live through a cancer that disfigured her face horrendously.

I couldn't envision a book about the body that didn't explore our sexuality. Can you imagine how your elbow might be sexy? Minnie Bruce Pratt will take you there. Stephen Dobyns writes of the sensuality of a high-school dance, something you may know about. There are two poems about kissing—one by Sir Philip Sidney from the sixteenth century and one by Marie Howe from the twenty-first. When Francisco Alarcón writes about a bridge, it's not the kind you drive over; he's expressing his passion for his lover. And when Lucille Clifton says, "these are big hips . . . ," she is not apologizing. We'll also consider the blurred lines that gender can have in an excerpt from Virginia Woolf's novel *Orlando*.

Hunger is not just a personal thing; it can be political— as shown by Miguel Hernández in his poem. We'll also take a look at William J. Harris's "Rib Sandwich." You'll see that his desire for ribs gave him more than something to eat, because culture is deeply connected to food. So when we sit down to dinner, we're feeding more than our stomachs. What we eat may say a lot about who we are and where we come from.

The body is not only life, but also death, and we'll see it through to that end. Gary Young witnesses a light very few of us will ever glimpse. Miller Williams writes about the loss of a friend to AIDS.

In life we have the opportunity to come to terms not only with an inner self, but also with the outer one. We'll look at how the two work together, and how we view the inside and the outside of other people. The body and the mind cohabitate, hence this book of poems about who the body is, what the body does, how we feel and what we think about it. Here are poems to comfort and surprise you and, perhaps, influence your idea of beauty. Your one body, the one whose hands hold this book, whose eyes read these words, is yours from birth to death.

PATRICE VECCHIONE

From **I Sing the Body Electric**

I

I sing the body electric,
The armies of those I love engirth me and I engirth them,
They will not let me off till I go with them, respond to
them,
And discorrupt them, and charge them full with the
charge of the soul.

Was it doubted that those who corrupt their own bodies
conceal themselves?
And if those who defile the living are as bad as they who
defile the dead?
And if the body does not do fully as much as the soul?
And if the body were not the soul, what is the soul?

2

The love of the body of man or woman balks account,
the body itself balks account,
That of the male is perfect, and that of the female is
perfect.

The expression of the face balks account,
But the expression of a well-made man appears not only
in his face,
It is in his limbs and joints also, it is curiously in the
joints of his hips and wrists,
It is in his walk, the carriage of his neck, the flex of his
waist and knees, dress does not hide him,

The strong sweet quality he has strikes through the
    cotton and broadcloth,
To see him pass conveys as much as the best poem,
    perhaps more,
You linger to see his back, and the back of his neck and
    shoulder-side.

The sprawl and fulness of babes, the bosoms and heads
    of women, the folds of their dress, their style as we
    pass in the street, the contour of their shape
    downwards,
The swimmer naked in the swimming-bath, seen as he
    swims through the transparent green-shine, or lies
    with his face up and rolls silently to and fro in the
    heave of the water,
The bending forward and backward of rowers in
    row-boats, the horseman in his saddle,
Girls, mothers, house-keepers, in all their performances,
The group of laborers seated at noon-time with their
    open dinner-kettles, and their wives waiting,
The female soothing a child, the farmer's daughter in the
    garden or cow-yard,
The young fellow hoeing corn, the sleigh-driver driving
    his six horses through the crowd,
The wrestle of wrestlers, two apprentice-boys, quite
    grown, lusty, good-natured, native-born, out on the
    vacant lot at sundown after work,
The coats and caps thrown down, the embrace of love
    and resistance,
The upper-hold and under-hold, the hair rumpled over
    and blinding the eyes;

The march of firemen in their own costumes, the play of
    masculine muscle through clean-setting trowsers and
    waist-straps,
The slow return from the fire, the pause when the bell
    strikes suddenly again, and the listening on the alert,
The natural, perfect, varied attitudes, the bent head, the
    curv'd neck and the counting;
Such-like I love—I loosen myself, pass freely, am at the
    mother's breast with the little child,
Swim with the swimmers, wrestle with wrestlers, march
    in line with the firemen, and pause, listen, count.

WALT WHITMAN

Planting Initiation Song

I have made a footprint, a sacred one.
I have made a footprint, through it the blades push
upward.
I have made a footprint, through it the blades radiate.
I have made a footprint, over it the blades float in the
wind.
I have made a footprint, over it I bend the stalk to pluck
the ears.
I have made a footprint, over it the blossoms lie gray.
I have made a footprint, smoke arises from my house.
I have made a footprint, there is cheer in my house.
I have made a footprint, I live in the light of day.

TRADITIONAL SONG OF THE OSAGE PEOPLE
(Translated by Francis La Flesche)

Little Clown, My Heart

Little clown, my heart,
Spangled again and lopsided,
Handstands and Peking pirouettes,
Backflips snapping open like
A carpenter's hinged ruler,

Little gimp-footed hurray,
Paper parasol of pleasures,
Fleshy undertongue of sorrows,
Sweet potato plant of my addictions,

Acapulco cliff-diver *corazón*,
Fine as an obsidian dagger,
Alley-oop and here we go
Into the froth, my life,
Into the flames!

SANDRA CISNEROS

Breath

You come to me from the oldest wound of wind
traveling like a long breath across the globe
through the full July moon of a hundred sleepless nights
and centuries of dew.

You come to me from mountains
bathed by powerful, musky angels,
through the scarred throat of fog
and archways drizzled with twilight.

You come to me from minarets
rising smoothly from sky to sky
through voices of muezzins
and parched pilgrims.

You come to me from rows and rows of orange trees
rows and rows of lemon trees
rows and rows of olive trees

from the smell of sleepy earth in my love's hair
from the call to prayer at 5 a.m.
from spreading my fingers over the scars of apple trees
from hummingbirds that race into the buds of fuchsia.

Not so long ago,
you showed me how the air grows soft
when the sun crawls from rock to cloud.
Not so long ago,
you showed me the stillness of death.

And I would pray to everything sacred
and I would bow and stare deeply at the earth
and walk through old cemeteries to find the dead
softly gazing.

Sometimes, I see the beautiful broken fighter
and his lonely mother
and I see you breathe red poppies over the hills
    in Palestine
and I see girls with orchards of almond trees in their eyes
and old men strolling silently
among fallen villages.

And I can't say how I love my people
and I can't tell my love how to leave our land without
    weeping
and I can't always love this land.

People who sit by the sea
find you there through the rough water.
Others see you in the faraway crescent moon,
only to find you breakfasting at their table.
Some yearn for years
and suddenly catch you in the deepest edges of their
    children's eyes.

DEEMA K. SHEHABI

A Dialogue

Says Body to Mind, ''Tis amazing to see,
We're so nearly related yet never agree,
But lead a most wrangling strange sort of a life,
As great plagues to each other as husband and wife.
The fault's all your own, who, with flagrant oppression,
Encroach every day on my lawful possession.
The best room in my house you have seized for your own,
And turned the whole tenement quite upside down,
While you hourly call in a disorderly crew
Of vagabond rogues, who have nothing to do
But to run in and out, hurry-scurry, and keep
Such a horrible uproar, I can't get to sleep.
There's my kitchen sometimes is as empty as sound,
I call for my servants, not one's to be found:
They all are sent out on your ladyship's errand,
To fetch some more riotous guests in, I warrant!
And since things are growing, I see, worse and worse,
I'm determined to force you to alter your course.'

Poor Mind, who heard all with extreme moderation,
Thought it now time to speak, and make her allegation:
''Tis I that, methinks, have most cause to complain,
Who am cramped and confined like a slave in a chain.
I did but step out, on some weighty affairs,
To visit, last night, my good friends in the stars,
When, before I was got half as high as the moon,
You despatched Pain and Languor to hurry me down;
Vi & Armis they seized me, in midst of my flight,
And shut me in caverns as dark as the night.'

''Twas no more,' replied Body, 'than what you deserved;
While you rambled abroad, I at home was half starved:
And, unless I had closely confined you in hold,
You had left me to perish with hunger and cold.'

'I've a friend,' answers Mind, 'who, though slow,
    is yet sure,
And will rid me at last of your insolent power:
Will knock down your walls, the whole fabric demolish,
And at once your strong holds and my slavery abolish:
And while in the dust your dull ruins decay,
I'll snap off my chains and fly freely away.'

ELIZABETH CARTER

Sudden Journey

Maybe I'm seven in the open field—
the straw-grass so high
only the top of my head makes a curve
of brown in the yellow. Rain then.
First a little. A few drops on my
wrist, the right wrist. More rain.
My shoulders, my chin. Until I'm looking up
to let my eyes take the bliss.
I open my face. Let the teeth show. I
pull my shirt down past the collar-bones.
I'm still a boy under my breast spots.
I can drink anywhere. The rain. My
skin shattering. Up suddenly, needing
to gulp, turning with my tongue, my arms out
running, running in the hard, cold plenitude
of all those who reach earth by falling.

TESS GALLAGHER

Black Hair

At eight I was brilliant with my body.
In July, that ring of heat
We all jumped through, I sat in the bleachers
Of Romain Playground, in the lengthening
Shade that rose from our dirty feet.
The game before us was more than baseball.
It was a figure—Hector Moreno
Quick and hard with turned muscles,
His crouch the one I assumed before an altar
Of worn baseball cards, in my room.

I came here because I was Mexican, a stick
Of brown light in love with those
Who could do it—the triple and hard slide,
The gloves eating balls into double plays.
What could I do with 50 pounds, my shyness,
My black torch of hair, about to go out?
Father was dead, his face no longer
Hanging over the table or our sleep,
And mother was the terror of mouths
Twisting hurt by butter knives.

In the bleachers I was brilliant with my body,
Waving players in and stomping my feet,
Growing sweaty in the presence of white shirts.
I chewed sunflower seeds. I drank water
And bit my arm through the late innings.
When Hector lined balls into deep

Center, in my mind I rounded the bases
With him, my face flared, my hair lifting
Beautifully, because we were coming home
To the arms of brown people.

GARY SOTO

Cobwebs

I walked around in my mother's high heels
I put her stockings over my head
ran my fingers over the black shiny beads
on her evening bag before she went out

I loved going through my mother's wooden bureau
top drawer was shallow with partitions
purses, gloves, hankies, and a gold cigarette lighter
with a built-in watch
the second drawer to the right   was deeper
underpants and bras
scented with smooth round bars of pale soap
a rubber disc inside a round box of bath powder
looked like a tiny trampoline or a yarmulke
I thought it was there to keep the powder   fresh

from the Fuller Brush man
there was an ivory colored oval hand mirror
it was so heavy I had to use both fists
to hold it up

In the second drawer to the left were slips and nighties
perfume blue and barely pink
I plunged my arms up to my elbows
in soft folded petals of my mother
I fingered the tiny rosebud
that floated on her necklines
summer nighties blizzarded with flowers
slippery thin straps   I liked best

the ones that were most worn   when she wore them
she looked like she was dressed in sheets of rain
I watched her blurry through the sliding glass
door in the shower   blindly washing her hair

When it was time for a bath
she squeezed ivory liquid under the tap
and put two or three of us   naked
into the tub
rising suds   our beards and mustaches

she threw in her stockings

we played till our fingers shriveled
we played till our lips turned blue.

MELINDA GOODMAN

The Gift

To pull the metal splinter from my palm
my father recited a story in a low voice.
I watched his lovely face and not the blade.
Before the story ended, he'd removed
the iron sliver I thought I'd die from.

I can't remember the tale,
but hear his voice still, a well
of dark water, a prayer.
And I recall his hands,
two measures of tenderness
he laid against my face,
the flames of discipline
he raised above my head.

Had you entered that afternoon
you would have thought you saw a man
planting something in a boy's palm,
a silver tear, a tiny flame.
Had you followed that boy
you would have arrived here,
where I bend over my wife's right hand.

Look how I shave her thumbnail down
so carefully she feels no pain.
Watch as I lift the splinter out.
I was seven when my father
took my hand like this,
and I did not hold that shard

between my fingers and think,
Metal that will bury me,
christen it Little Assassin,
Ore Going Deep for My Heart.
And I did not lift up my wound and cry,
Death visited here!
I did what a child does
when he's given something to keep.
I kissed my father.

LI-YOUNG LEE

Self-Portrait, 1906

The stamina of an old, long-noble race
in the eyebrows' heavy arches. In the mild
blue eyes, the solemn anguish of a child
and, here and there, humility—not a fool's,
but feminine: the look of one who serves.
The mouth quite ordinary, large and straight,
composed, yet not unwilling to speak out
when necessary. The forehead still naive,
most comfortable in shadows, looking down.

This, as a whole, just hazily foreseen—
never, in any joy or suffering,
collected for a firm accomplishment;
and yet, as though, from far off, with scattered Things,
a serious, true work were being planned.

RAINER MARIA RILKE
(Translated from the German by Stephen Mitchell)

From Autobiography of a Face

I spent five years of my life being treated for cancer, but since then I've spent fifteen years being treated for nothing other than looking different from everyone else. It was the pain from that, from feeling ugly, that I always viewed as the great tragedy in my life. The fact that I had cancer seemed minor in comparison.

The journey back to my face was a long one. Between operations, thanks to some unexpected money inherited from my grandmother, I traveled around Europe. I kept writing. I returned to Berlin and sat in the same cafés as before, but now without my image, without the framework of *when my face gets fixed, then I'll start living.* I felt there was something empty about me. I didn't tell anyone, not my sister, not my closest friends, that I had stopped looking in mirrors. I found that I could stare straight through a mirror, allowing none of the reflection to get back to me.

Unlike some stroke victims, who are physically unable to name the person in the mirror as themselves, my trick of the eye was the result of my lifelong refusal to learn *how* to name the person in the mirror. My face had been changing for so long that I had never had time to become acquainted with it, to develop anything other than an ephemeral relationship with it. It was easy for me to ascribe to physical beauty certain qualities that I thought I simply had to wait for. It was easier to think that I was still not beautiful enough or lovable enough than to admit that perhaps these qualities did not really belong to this thing I thought was called beauty after all.

Without another operation to hang all my hopes on, I was completely on my own. And now something inside me started to miss me. A part of me, one that had always been there, organically *knew* I was whole. It was as if this part had known it was necessary to wait so long, to wait until the impatient din around it had quieted down, until the other internal voices had grown exhausted and hoarse before it could begin to speak, before I would begin to listen.

LUCY GREALY

Scars

They tell how it was, and how time
came along, and how it happened
again and again. They tell
the slant life takes when it turns
and slashes your face as a friend.

Any wound is real. In church
a woman lets the sun find
her cheek, and we see the lesson:
there are years in that book; there are sorrows
a choir can't reach when they sing.

Rows of children lift their faces of promise,
places where the scars will be.

WILLIAM STAFFORD

Olivia's Face,
from Twelfth Night

VIOLA: 'Tis beauty truly blent, whose red and white
    Nature's own sweet and cunning hand laid on.
    Lady, you are the cruell'st she alive,
    If you will lead these graces to the grave,
    And leave the world no copy.

OLIVIA: O, sir, I will not be so hard-hearted; I will give out
    divers schedules of my beauty. It shall be inventoried,
    and every particle and utensil labell'd to my will: as—
    item, two lips indifferent red; item, two grey eyes with
    lids to them; item, one neck, one chin, and so forth.
    Were you sent hither to praise me?

WILLIAM SHAKESPEARE

Doreen

Doreen had a round face.
She tried to change it.
Everybody made fun
of her in school.

Her eyes so narrow
they asked if she could see,
called her Moonface and
Slits.

Doreen frost tipped her hair,
ratted it five inches high,
painted her eyes round,
glittering blue shadow up to her brow.

Made her look sad
even when she smiled.

She cut gym all the time
because the white powder on her neck
and face would streak
when she sweat.

But Doreen had boobs
more than most of us Japanese girls
so she wore tight sweaters
and low cut dresses
even in winter.

She didn't hang
with us,
since she put so much time
into changing her face.

White boys
would snicker when she passed by
and word got around
that Doreen
went all the way,
smoked and drank beer.

She told us
she met a veteran
fresh back from Korea.

Fresh back
his leg
still puckered pink
from landmines.

She told us
it was a kick
to listen to his stories
about how they'd torture
the gooks
hang them from trees
by their feet
grenades
in their crotch
and watch
them sweat.

I asked her
why she didn't dig brothers.

And her eyes
would disappear
laughing
so loud
she couldn't hear herself.

One day,
Doreen riding fast
with her friend
went through the windshield
and tore off
her skin
from scalp to chin.

And we were sad.

Because
no one could remember
Doreen's face.

JANICE MIRIKITANI

We Wear the Mask

We wear the mask that grins and lies,
It hides our cheeks and shades our eyes,—
This debt we pay to human guile;
With torn and bleeding hearts we smile,
And mouth with myriad subtleties.

Why should the world be overwise,
In counting all our tears and sighs?
Nay, let them only see us, while
    We wear the mask.

We smile, but, O great Christ, our cries
To thee from tortured souls arise.
We sing, but oh the clay is vile
Beneath our feet, and long the mile;
But let the world dream otherwise,
    We wear the mask!

PAUL LAURENCE DUNBAR

They Lied

for Katherine

They lied, my friend. They injected
their despair beneath your skin
like a parasitic insect laying eggs
in the body of another species.

Nothing they said is true,
everything about you is honorable. Every pore
that opens and closes—a multitude
along the expanse of your body, the
follicles from which hair sprouts
emerging again and again like spiders' floss
spun from a limitless source.

Your feet with thickened nails. Your anger
like the wisdom of elephants. Your
omnipresent fear, like mist off the sea.
Your neglected breasts and the sober practicality
of the anus. Your elegant neck and
quick smile. Your small hungers,
each a song.

You wait, huddled. Or carry yourself from
place to place like a burden. As if
you would stash yourself, if you could,
in a bus station locker, or somewhere smaller.
You don't really hope, but
you can't give it up completely.

Some stubborn nugget
is lodged like a bullet in bone.
Though each breath stings with the cold
suck of it, you can know the truth.
Every cell of your body vibrates with its own intelligence.
Every atom is pure.

ELLEN BASS

A Hand

A hand is not four fingers and a thumb.

Nor is it palm and knuckles,
not ligaments or the fat's yellow pillow,
not tendons, star of the wristbone, meander of veins.

A hand is not the thick thatch of its lines
with their infinite dramas,
nor what it has written,
not on the page,
not on the ecstatic body.

Nor is the hand its meadows of holding, of shaping—
not sponge of rising yeast-bread,
not rotor pin's smoothness,
not ink.

The maple's green hands do not cup
the proliferant rain.
What empties itself falls into the place that is open.

A hand turned upwards holds only a single, transparent
    question.

Unanswerable, humming like bees, it rises, swarms,
    departs.

JANE HIRSHFIELD

The Nailbiter

Some people manicure their nails,
Some people trim them neatly,
Some people keep them filed down,
I bite 'em off completely.
Yes, it's a nasty habit, but
Before you start to scold,
Remember, I have never ever
Scratched a single soul.

SHEL SILVERSTEIN

His Hands

His hands will never be large enough.
Not for the woman who sees in his face
the father she can't remember,
or her first husband, the soldier with two wives—
all the men who would only take.
Not large enough to deflect
the sharp edges of her words.

Still he tries to prove himself in work,
his callused hands heaving crates
all day on the docks, his pay twice spent.
He brings home what he can, buckets of crabs
from his morning traps, a few green bananas.

His supper waits in the warming oven,
the kitchen dark, the screens hooked.
He thinks, *make the hands gentle*
as he raps lightly on the back door.
He has never had a key.

Putting her hands to his, she pulls him in,
sets him by the stove. Slowly, she rubs oil
into his cracked palms, drawing out soreness
from the swells, removing splinters, taking
whatever his hands will give.

NATASHA TRETHEWEY

Making Tortillas

for Liliana, "la Argentina"

My body remembers
what it means to love slowly,
what it means to start
from scratch:
to soak the maíz,
scatter bonedust in the limewater,
and let the seeds soften
overnight.

Sunrise is the best time
for grinding masa,
cornmeal rolling out
on the metate like a flannel sheet.
Smell of wet corn, lard, fresh
morning love and the light
sound of clapping.

                    Pressed between the palms,
    clap-clap
                    thin yellow moons—
    clap-clap
                    still moist, heavy still
                    from last night's soaking
    clap-clap
                    slowly start finding their shape
    clap-clap.

My body remembers
the feel of the griddle,

beads of grease sizzling
under the skin, a cry gathering
like an air bubble in the belly
of the unleavened cake. Smell
of baked tortillas all over the house,
all over the hands still
hot from clapping, cooking.
Tortilleras, we are called,
grinders of maíz, makers, bakers,
slow lovers of women.
The secret is starting from scratch.

ALICIA GASPAR DE ALBA

Rib Sandwich

I wanted a rib sandwich

So I got into my car
and drove as fast as I could
to a little black restaurant-
bar
and walked in
and so doing
walked out
of
America

and didn't even
need a passport

WILLIAM J. HARRIS

Hunger

Keep hunger in mind: remember its past
trampled with foremen who pay you in lead.
That wage is paid in blood received,
with a yoke on the soul, and blows to the back.

Hunger paraded its caved-in cows,
its dried-up women, its devoured teats,
its gaping jawbones, its miserable lives
past the strapping bodies of all the eaters.

The abundant years, the satiety, the glut
were only for those who get called boss.
I am here, we are here, to make sure that bread
goes straight to the teeth of the hungry poor.

Maybe we can't be those at the front
who understand life as bloody war-booty:
like sharks, all greed and tooth,
or eager panthers in a world always starving.

Years of hunger have been, for the poor, the only years.
Quantities of bread were heaped up for others,
and hunger wolfed down its ravenous flocks
of crows, clawed things, wolves, scorpions.

I fight, famished, will all my gashes,
scars and wounds, souvenirs and memories

of hunger, against all those smug bellies:
hogs who were born more lowly than hogs.

For having engorged yourselves so basely and brutally,
wallowing deeper than pigs at play,
you will be plunged into this huge current
of blazing spikes, of menacing fists.

You have not wanted to open your ears to hear
the weeping of millions of young workers.
You just pay lip service, when hunger comes to the door
begging with the mouths of the very stars.

In every house: hatred, like a grove of fig trees,
like a quaking bull with shaking horns
breaking loose from the barn, circling, waiting,
and doing you in on its horns as you agonize like dogs.

II
Hunger is the most important thing to know:
to be hungry is the first lesson we learn.
And the ferocity of what you feel,
there where the stomach begins, sets you on fire.

You aren't quite human if, when you strangle
doves one day you don't have a bad conscience:
if you can't drown doves in cold snow,
who know nothing, if not innocence.

The animal is a huge influence on me,
a beast roars through all my strength, my passions.

Sometimes I have to make the greatest effort
to calm the voice of the lion in me.

I am proud to own the animal in my life,
but in the animal, the human persists.
And I look for my body as the purest thing
to nest in such a jungle, with its basic courage.

Through hunger, man re-enters the labyrinth
where life is lived sinister, and alone.
The beast turns up again, recaptures its instincts,
its bristling paws, its animus, its tail.

Learning and wisdom are thrown out,
your mask is removed, the skin of culture,
the eyes of science, the recent crust
of knowledge that reveals and procures things.

Then you know only evil, extermination.
You invent gases, launch ruinous ideas,
return to the cloven hoof, regress to the kingdom
of the fang, dominate the big eaters.

You train the beast, clutch the ladle,
ready for anybody who comes near the table.
Then I see over the whole world only a troop
of tigers, and the sorry sight aches in my eyes.

I haven't opened my soul to so much tiger,
adopted so much of the jackal, that the wine I feel,
the bread, the day, the hunger isn't shared
with other hungers fed nobly into my mouth.

Help me to be a man: don't let me be a beast,
starving, enraged, forever cornered.
A common animal, with working blood,
I give you the humanity that this song foretells.

MIGUEL HERNÁNDEZ
(Translated from the Spanish by Don Share)

Eating the Pig

Twelve people, most of us strangers, stand in a room
in Ann Arbor, drinking Cribari from jars.
Then two young men, who cooked him,
carry him to the table
on a large square of plywood: his body
striped, like a tiger cat's, from the basting,
his legs long, much longer than a cat's,
and the striped hide as shiny as vinyl.

Now I see his head, as he takes his place
at the center of the table,
his wide pig's head; and he looks like the *javelina*
that ran in front of the car, in the desert outside Tucson,
and I am drawn to him, my brother the pig,
with his large ears cocked forward,
with his tight snout, with his small ferocious teeth
in a jaw propped open
by an apple. How bizarre, this raw apple clenched,
in a cooked face! Then I see his eyes,
his eyes cramped shut, his no-eyes, his eyes like X's
in a comic strip, when the character gets knocked out.

This afternoon they read directions
from a book: *The eyeballs must be removed
or they will burst during roasting.*   So they hacked them out.
"I nearly fainted," says someone.
"I never fainted before, in my whole life."

Then they gutted the pig and stuffed him,
and roasted him five hours, basting the long body.

2

Now we examine him, exclaiming, and we marvel at him—
but no one picks up a knife.

Then a young woman cuts off his head.
It comes off so easily, like a detachable part.
With sudden enthusiasm we dismantle the pig,
we wrench his trotters off, we twist them
at shoulder and hip, and they come off so easily.
Then we cut open his belly and pull the skin back.

For myself, I scoop a portion of left thigh,
moist, tender, falling apart, fat, sweet.

. . .

We forage like an army starving in winter
that crosses a pass in the hills and discovers
a valley of full barns—
cattle fat and lowing in their stalls,
bins of potatoes in root cellars under white farmhouses,
barrels of cider, onions, hens squawking over eggs—
and the people nowhere, with bread still warm in the oven.

Maybe, south of the valley, refugees pull their carts
listening for Stukas or elephants, carrying
bedding, pans, and silk dresses,
old men and women, children, deserters, young wives.

No, we are here, eating the pig together.

3

In ten minutes, the destruction is total.

His tiny ribs, delicate as birds' feet, lie crisscrossed.
Or they are like cross-hatching in a drawing,
lines doubling and redoubling on each other.
Bits of fat and muscle
mix with stuffing alien to the body,
walnuts and plums. His skin, like a parchment bag
soaked in oil, is pulled back and flattened,
with ridges and humps remaining, like a contour map,
like the map of a defeated country.

The army consumes every blade of grass in the valley,
every tree, every stream, every village,
every crossroad, every shack, every book, every graveyard.

. . .

His intact head
swivels around, to view the landscape of body
as if in dismay.

"For sixteen weeks I lived. For sixteen weeks
I took into myself nothing but the milk of my mother
who rolled on her side for me,
for my brothers and sisters. Only five hours roasting,
and this body so quickly dwindles away to nothing."

4

By itself, isolated on this plywood,
among this puzzle of foregone possibilities,

his intact head seems to want affection.
Without knowing that I will do it,
I reach out and scratch his jaw,
and I stroke him behind his ears,
as if he might suddenly purr from his cooked head.

"When I stroke your pig's ears,
and scratch the striped leather of your jowls,
the furrow between the sockets of your eyes,
I take into myself, and digest,
wheat
that grew between
the Tigris and the Euphrates rivers.

"And I take into myself the flint carving tool,
and the savannah, and hairs in the tail
of Eohippus, and fingers of bamboo,
and Hannibal's elephant, and Hannibal,
and everything that lived before us, everything born,
exalted, and dead, and historians
who carved in the Old Kingdom
when the wall had not heard about China."

I speak these words
into the ear of the stone-age pig, the Abraham
pig, the ocean pig, the Achilles pig,
and into the ears
of the fire pig that will eat our bodies up.

"Fire, brother and father,
twelve of us, in our different skins, older and younger,

opened your skin together
and tore your body apart, and took it
into our bodies."

DONALD HALL

Fat

Some of it I've
given away, I guess that
comes from thinking
nobody could
want it.
Fat. Something you
take in and just
can't use.
It hangs around
reminding you of what
wasn't totally
digested, a layer of heavy
water, grease

having so
much I'd dream the
4:30 tall thin
shadow thighs were
me, pressed so hard it
hurt, a
punishment squeezing
myself into
me, into
what I didn't
want. Afternoons
with the shades drawn
examining and hating what

I saw, longing for one of those
svelte bodies

I put the
scales back, would have
beat myself with
rubber chains

when I was 12 I bought a
rubber girdle, nobody
knew I peeled it off with the
door locked

Somebody once said
you'll never get
cold this winter
fat legs
like that

How could something like fat ever
protect you from anything
outside being only an
extension of yourself, cells
spreading, making you
more vulnerable,
fat people having more
places to bruise
or scar

I sat in a room and
watched the
river when

other girls
were going across the
state line,
were necking in cars at
Lake Bomoseen
despising those
layers I
didn't need

belly that
I hated and squeezed into
clothes a size
too small, hips, but
worse, thighs I
hated them
most, spreading out
on benches
for basketball practice

Once I lay on my
back cycling air until
the room spun

white waves of the body
I was so ashamed I wouldn't go
to the beach

my mother always
said *Yes, you're pretty*
eat and I curled
into myself

eating what made
me worse

tho I wanted to
wear pleats
and be delicate

In one store a
man asked her
is it difficult
having one daughter
who's so lovely? and I
hated my sister for being
blond, her body
like a Keene
waif, I was jealous of
her eggnogs and
chocolate
how meat had to be
coaxed to her
bones

You can't camouflage
hold anything in
that long, it explodes
a rubber girdle pops
elastic
letting go
then they know
that there's more
than you can
handle.

look at me now and
you say *but those*
thin wrists

Listen when I weigh
over a hundred I
break out in
hives. We

all think of our
selves the way
we were

especially when it
comes to what we
don't love

Once when I was
walking home from
school the elastic
on my underpants died
The next day someone
wrote kike on the
blackboard
Both I knew were a result
of fat

I've never been good
at getting rid of
what I can't use
but that's when I
knew that I had to

that round face with
glasses, bulging
thighs. You know

when some man says
love it's still
hard to believe

If I wear my clothes
too short, it's to
remind myself (I still
avoid mirrors,
glass) that my

legs are not
unlovable, I

want you to see I finally am
someone you might
want to dance with
this me waiting under
neath on the
sidelines

years of
getting down to

But it really is
sweetest close
to the bone

LYN LIFSHIN

The Dieter's Daughter

Mom's got this taco guy's poem
taped to the fridge, some ode to celery,
which she is always eating.
The celery, I mean, not the poem
which talks about green angels
and fragile corsets. I don't get it,
but Mom says by the time she reads it
she forgets she's hungry. One stalk
for breakfast, along with half a grapefruit,
or a glass of aloe vera juice,
you know that stuff that comes from cactus,
and one stalk for lunch
with some protein drink
that tastes like dried placenta,
did you know that they put cow placenta
in make-up, face cream, stuff like that?
Yuck. Well, Mom says it's never too early
to wish you looked different,
which means I got to eat that crap too.
Mom says: your body is a temple,
not the place all good twinkies go to.
Mom says: that boys remember
girls that're slender.
Mom says that underneath all this fat
there's a whole new me,
one I'd really like if only I gave myself
the chance. Mom says: you are
what you eat, which is why she eats celery,
because she wants to be thin,

not green or stringy, of course—
am I talking too fast?—
but thin as paper
like the hearts we cut out
and send to ourselves,
don't tell anyone,
like the hearts of gold
melons we eat
down
to the bitter rind.

ANITA ENDREZZE

In the Morning

In the morning,
holding her mirror,
the young woman
touches
her tender
lip with
her finger &
then with
the tip of
her tongue
licks it &
smiles
& admires her
eyes.

STEVE KOWIT
(*After the Sanskrit*)

From Skinhead

They call me skinhead, and I got my own beauty.
It is knife-scrawled across my back in sure, jagged letters,
it's the way my eyes snap away from the obvious.
I sit in my dim matchbox,
on the edge of a bed tousled with my ragged smell,
slide razors across my hair,
count how many ways
I can bring blood closer to the surface of my skin.
These are the duties of the righteous,
the ways of the anointed.

The face that moves in my mirror is huge and
　　pockmarked,
scraped pink and brilliant, apple-cheeked,
I am filled with my own spit.

PATRICIA SMITH

She Walks in Beauty

1

She walks in beauty, like the night
    Of cloudless climes and starry skies;
And all that's best of dark and bright
    Meet in her aspect and her eyes:
Thus mellowed to that tender light
    Which heaven to gaudy day denies.

2

One shade the more, one ray the less,
    Had half impaired the nameless grace
Which waves in every raven tress,
    Or softly lightens o'er her face;
Where thoughts serenely sweet express
    How pure, how dear their dwelling place.

3

And on that cheek, and o'er that brow,
    So soft, so calm, yet eloquent,
The smiles that win, the tints that glow,
    But tell of days in goodness spent,
A mind at peace with all below,
    A heart whose love is innocent!

GEORGE GORDON, LORD BYRON

Possible

It is the breast I remember seeing,
the nipple pink and round, the lustrous flesh,
before I saw the woman had no arms
in the locker room. Her teeth were excellent,
tugging her blouse on,

but it is her breast I remember
when I see again how what is perfect
lives beside what is tragic and damaged,
how silence arcs between these two,
each making the other possible.

RUTH L. SCHWARTZ

Height

Like bamboo
I only look fragile
bend,
but do not break
sway dangerously close to
the ground in painful angles
do not break
stand straight
stretch high
face closer to the sun
this time
hair tangling up the stars
this time
do not break
do not merely
bounce back
bend
low
and not always graceful
but taller
always taller
when I choose to stand again.

MARIAHADESSA EKERE TALLIE

From Alice's Adventures in Wonderland

"Curiouser and curiouser!" cried Alice (she was so much surprised, that for the moment she quite forgot how to speak good English); "now I'm opening out like the largest telescope that ever was! Good-bye, feet!" (for when she looked down at her feet, they seemed to be almost out of sight, they were getting so far off) "Oh, my poor little feet, I wonder who will put on your shoes and stockings for you now, dears? I'm sure I shan't be able! I shall be a great deal too far off to trouble myself about you: you must manage the best way you can;—but I must be kind to them," thought Alice, "or perhaps they won't walk the way I want to go! Let me see: I'll give them a new pair of boots every Christmas."

And she went on planning to herself how she would manage it. "They must go by the carrier," she thought; "and how funny it'll seem, sending presents to one's own feet! And how odd the directions will look!

> Alice's Right Foot, Esq.
>> Hearthrug,
>>> near the Fender,
>>>> (with Alice's love.)

Oh dear, what nonsense I'm talking!"

Just at this moment her head struck against the roof of the hall: in fact she was now rather more than nine feet high, and she at once took up the little golden key and hurried off to the garden door.

Poor Alice! It was as much as she could do, lying down on one side, to look through into the garden with one eye;

but to get through was more hopeless than ever: she sat down and began to cry again.

"You ought to be ashamed of yourself," said Alice, "a great girl like you," (she might well say this,) "to go on crying in this way! Stop this moment, I tell you!" But she went on all the same, shedding gallons of tears, until there was a large pool all round her, about four inches deep and reaching half down the hall. . . .

"Dear, dear! How queer everything is to-day! And yesterday things went on just as usual. I wonder if I've been changed in the night? Let me think: was I the same when I got up this morning? I almost think I can remember feeling a little different. But if I'm not the same, the next question is, Who in the world am I? Ah, *that's* the great puzzle!"

LEWIS CARROLL

A Breast for All Seasons

They were "Jugs" in fifth grade.
Spoken by a smirk,
a boy who knew of sex
from dogs and bathroom Playboys.

In fourth grade they demanded attention,
stood for duty, and erect salute.
They were a mesmerizing lieutenant,
a foot below my eyes.
Boys were hypnotized in awe,
lost in the valley, over the crest,
swallowed by size.

They were a neon sign saying,
"Yes, we are open for business."
They were an awning, a bellboy
guarding my front door.

These ornaments on my chest,
this grip I offer in passion,
these balls of fat and gland,
My treasure chest, My fifth pocket,
My nectar, My sweet-tits;
A pair of pants I've grown into,
a bike I'm ready to ride.

KEELYN T. HEALY

Pastel Dresses

Like a dream, which when one
becomes conscious of it
becomes a confusion, so her name
slipped between the vacancies.

As little more than a child
I hurried among the phalanx
of rowdy boys across a dance floor—
such a clattering of black shoes.

Before us sat a row of girls
in pastel dresses waiting.
One sat to the right. I uttered
some clumsy grouping of sounds.

She glanced up to where I stood
and the brightness of her eyes
made small explosions within me.
That's all that's left.

I imagine music, an evening,
a complete story, but truly
there is only her smile and my response—
warm fingerprints crowding my chest.

A single look like an inch of canvas
cut from a painting: the shy complicity,
the expectation of pleasure, the eager
pushing forward into the mystery.

Maybe I was fourteen. Pressed
to the windows, night bloomed
in the alleyways and our futures
rushed off like shafts of light.

My hand against the small of a back,
the feel of a dress, that touch
of starched fabric, its damp warmth—
was that her or some other girl?

Scattered fragments, scattered faces—
the way a breeze at morning
disperses mist across a pond,
so the letters of her name

return to the alphabet. Her eyes,
were they gray? How can we not love
this world for what it gives us? How
can we not hate it for what it takes away?

STEPHEN DOBYNS

homage to my hips

these hips are big hips.
they need space to
move around in.
they don't fit into little
petty places. these hips
are free hips.
they don't like to be held back.
these hips have never been enslaved,
they go where they want to go
they do what they want to do.
these hips are mighty hips.
these hips are magic hips.
i have known them
to put a spell on a man and
spin him like a top!

LUCILLE CLIFTON

Elbows

Cover your arms.
Don't let your elbows
show.

That's what my neighbors
down in Alabama tell
their daughters
so no elbow
plump or thin
tan or pink
will entice others
to passion.

But if I thought
my scrawny, two-toned
elbows would lure you

if I thought
my skinny, sharp-boned
elbows could secure you

I'd flap my arms
like a chicken
like a peafowl
like a guinea hen

when next I saw you
honey
I'd roll

up my sleeves and
sin
sin
sin.

MINNIE BRUCE PRATT

Your Laughter

Take bread away from me, if you wish,
take air away, but
do not take from me your laughter.

Do not take away the rose,
the lanceflower that you pluck,
the water that suddenly
bursts forth in your joy,
the sudden wave
of silver born in you.

My struggle is harsh and I come back
with eyes tired
at times from having seen
the unchanging earth,
but when your laughter enters
it rises to the sky seeking me
and it opens for me all
the doors of life.

My love, in the darkest
hour your laughter
opens, and if suddenly
you see my blood staining
the stones of the street,
laugh, because your laughter
will be for my hands
like a fresh sword.

Next to the sea in the autumn,
your laughter must raise
its foamy cascade,
and in the spring, love,
I want your laughter like
the flower I was waiting for,
the blue flower, the rose
of my echoing country.

Laugh at the night,
at the day, at the moon,
laugh at the twisted
streets of the island,
laugh at this clumsy
boy who loves you,
but when I open
my eyes and close them,
when my steps go,
when my steps return,
deny me bread, air,
light, spring,
but never your laughter
for I would die.

PABLO NERUDA
(Translated from the Spanish by Donald Walsh)

Crying

Crying only a little bit
is no use. You must cry
until your pillow is soaked!
Then you can get up and laugh.
Then you can jump in the shower
and splash-splash-splash!
Then you can throw open your window
and, "Ha ha! ha ha!"
And if people say, "Hey,
what's going on up there?"
"Ha ha!" sing back, "Happiness
was hiding in the last tear!
I wept it! Ha ha!"

GALWAY KINNELL

Stella's Kiss

Sweet kiss, thy sweets I fain would sweetly indite
Which even of sweetness sweetest sweetener art,
Pleasingst consort, where each sense holds a part,
Which, coupling doves, guides Venus' chariot right;
Best charge and bravest retrait in Cupid's fight,
A double key which opens to the heart,
Most rich when most his riches it impart;
Nest of young joys, schoolmaster of delight,
Teaching the means at once to take and give;
The friendly fray, where blows both wound and heal,
The pretty death, while each in other live.
Poor hope's first wealth, hostage of promist weal,
Breakfast of love. But lo, lo, where she is,
Cease we to praise: now pray we for a kiss.

SIR PHILIP SIDNEY

The Kiss

When he finally put
his mouth on me—on

my shoulder—the world
shifted a little on the tilted

axis of itself. The minutes
since my brother died

stopped marching ahead like
dumb soldiers and

the stars rested.
His mouth on my shoulder and

then on my throat
and the world started up again

for me,
some machine deep inside it

recalibrating,
all the little wheels

slowly reeling and speeding up,
the massive dawn lifting on the other

side of the turning world.
And when his mouth

pressed against my
mouth, I

opened my mouth
and the world's chord

played at once:
a large, ordinary music rising

from a hand neither one of us could see.

MARIE HOWE

From Orlando

He called her a melon, a pineapple, an olive tree, an emerald, and a fox in the snow all in the space of three seconds; he did not know whether he had heard her, tasted her, seen her, or all three together. (For though we must pause not a moment in the narrative we may here hastily note that all his images at this time were simple in the extreme to match his senses and were mostly taken from things he had liked the taste of as a boy. But if his senses were simple they were at the same time extremely strong. To pause therefore and seek the reasons of things is out of the question.) . . . A melon, an emerald, a fox in the snow—so he raved, so he stared. When the boy, for alas, a boy it must be—no woman could skate with such speed and vigour—swept almost on tiptoe past him, Orlando was ready to tear his hair with vexation that the person was of his own sex, and thus all embraces were out of the question. But the skater came closer. Legs, hands, carriage, were a boy's, but no boy ever had a mouth like that; no boy had those breasts; no boy had eyes which looked as if they had been fished from the bottom of the sea. Finally, coming to a stop and sweeping a curtsey with the utmost grace to the King, who was shuffling past on the arm of some Lord-in-waiting, the unknown skater came to a standstill. She was not a handsbreadth off. She was a woman. Orlando stared; trembled; turned hot; turned cold; longed to hurl himself through the summer air; to crush acorns beneath his feet; to toss his arms with the beech trees and the oaks. As it was, he drew his lips up over his small white teeth; opened them perhaps half an inch as if to bite; shut them as if he had bitten.

VIRGINIA WOOLF

Bridge

extend
your arms
extend them
until your hands
touch the edge
of my body

I will travel
across your body
like someone
who crosses
a bridge
and saves himself

FRANCISCO X. ALARCÓN

Erections

When first described imperfectly
by my shy mother, I tried to leap

from the moving
car. A response,

I suspect, of not
just terror (although

a kind of terror continues to play
its part), but also a mimetic gesture,

the expression equal
to a body's system of absurd

jokes and dirty stories.
With cockeyed breasts

peculiar as distant cousins,
and already the butt of the body's

frat-boy humor,
I'd begun to pack

a bag, would set off
soon for my separate

country. Now, sometimes,
I admire the surprised engineering:

how a man's body can rise,
squaring off with the weight

of gravity, single-minded,
exposed as the blind

in traffic. It's the body leaping
that I praise, vulnerable

in empty space.
It's mapping the empty

space; a man's life driving
down a foreign road.

ERIN BELIEU

Semen

Because no words suffice for this cry
it lives as a blood-colored syllable.

And circles a ring of desire
like a cloudburst, sultry and dense:
red sulphate of quicklime, a secret sun
opening and closing the genital doors.

PABLO NERUDA
(Translated from the Spanish by Ben Belitt)

This Part of Your Body

to Annie at 12, beginning the menses

you won't touch it or call it by name yet
but this part of your body—
this part of your body
you're going to get to know
better than your elbow
this part of your body
you're going to love
and hate
this part of your body
will swell and drip dew
attracting hunters and slaves
this part of your body
may be your secret joy
but this part of your body
will keep you off the streets after dark
it will be poked and spread by stainless steel
scrutinized by strangers with scalpels
behind white drapes
as if it were not a part of you
this part of your body will stretch
over the heads of human beings
or tighten to a finger in its gentle rhythm
this part of your body
is more expressive
than your mouth
this part of your body
laughs louder
has its own exhausted grimace

this part of your body moans
its lonely emptiness
you will spend your life trying to fill
this part of your body

LIN MAX

The Moment

When I saw the dark Egyptian stain,
I went down into the house to find you, Mother—
past the grandfather clock, with its huge
ochre moon, past the burnt
sienna woodwork, rubbed and glazed.
I went deeper and deeper down into the
body of the house, down below the
level of the earth. It must have been
the maid's day off, for I found you there
where I had never found you, by the wash tubs,
your hands thrust deep in soapy water,
and above your head, the blazing windows
at the surface of the ground.
You looked up from the iron sink,
a small haggard pretty woman
of 40, one week divorced.
"I've got my period, Mom," I said,
and saw your face abruptly break open and
glow with joy. "Baby," you said,
coming toward me, hands out and
covered with tiny delicate bubbles like seeds.

SHARON OLDS

April

Suddenly, the legs want a different sort of work.
This is because the eyes look out the window
And the sight is filled with hope.
This is because the eyes look out the window

And the street looks a fraction better than the day before.
This is what the eyes tell the legs,
Whose joints become smeared with a fresh sap
Which would bud if attached to a different limb.

The legs want a different sort of work.
This is because the ears hear what they've been waiting for,
Which cannot be described in words,
But makes the heart beat faster, as if
One had just found money in the street.

The legs want to put on a show for the entire world.
The legs want to reclaim their gracefulness.
This is because the nose at last finds the right scent
And tugs the protesting body onto the dance floor.
This is because the hands, stretching out in boredom,
Accidentally brush against the skirts of the world.

CORNELIUS EADY

Heel should not be an insult

The true humility of heels:
pale, battered, wrinkled, swollen.
We may paint our toes, but naked
heels are dumb as cows' behinds.

Patient, stubborn, vulnerable
they follow us looking back
like children in cars making faces
through the rear view window.

In undressing a lover, even
foot fetishists must blink:
the sock, the stocking peeled,
the unappetizing bony fruit.

We are always landing on them
slamming them into pavement,
jumping out of trucks, forcing
them into stirrups and pedals.

Cats walk on their toes like ballerinas
but we, ape cousins, go shuffling
and what we leave in the sand
is the imprint of our heels coming home.

They are the periods under the leaping
exclamation point, gravity's mooring,
our anchor to earth, the callused
blind familiar of soil, rock, root.

Let me rub your angular barnacled
hull with unguents and massage you
tenderly, my little flatiron shaped
heroes, my hard laboring heels.

MARGE PIERCY

I Used to Be Much Much Darker

I used to be
much much darker
dark as la tierra
recién llovida
and dark was all
I ever wanted:
dark tropical
mountains
dark daring
eyes
dark tender lips
and I would sing
dark
dream dark
talk only dark

happiness
was to spend
whole
afternoons
tirado como foca
bajo el sol
"you're already
so dark
muy prieto
too indio!"
some would lash

at my happy
darkness but
I could only
smile back

now I'm not as
dark as I once was
quizás sean
los años
maybe I'm too
far up north
not enough sun
not enough time
but anyway
up here "dark"
is only for
the ashes
the stuff
lonely nights
are made of

FRANCISCO X. ALARCÓN

Skin Dreaming

Skin is the closest thing to god,
touching oil, clay,
intimate with the foreign land of air
and other bodies,
places not in light,
lonely
for its own image.

It is awash in its own light.
It wants to swim and surface
from the red curve of sea,
open all its eyes.

Skin is the oldest thing.
It remembers when it was the cold
builder of fire,
when darkness was the circle around it,
when there were eyes shining in the night,
a breaking twig, and it rises
in fear, a primitive lord on new bones.

I tell you, it is old,
it heals and is sometimes merciful.
It is water.
It has fallen through ancestral hands.
It is the bearer of vanished forest

fallen through teeth and jaws
of earth
where we were once other
visions and creations.

LINDA HOGAN

The skin of this poem

Before my parents made me,
sliding the long curve of Viet Nam
into the wide-hipped center
of the United States so that my skin

and hair and eyes were pale,
reddish blonde and bluish-green,
a sort of American flag of colors
wrapped around my narrow-shouldered

slender, long-legged bones,
Vietnamese bones
saved from bombing, flown
from burning by the grace of those

who made me; I wonder
did they know they were building
a child, a daughter
or son, with the tools

of their bodies, with the sperm
of his persistence, with her one
egg ripe with faith
for a future that might wait beyond

napalm, destruction,
the slow tick of herbicides,
cancer, loss, despair;
did I push off

from their bodies
with my own sweet allegiance, forged
from two countries at war, a man
and a woman, writing

the language of all survivors
into the skin of this poem;
my face, my name
one of many bridges forward,

faithful to the work of those who made me.

KIM LY BUI-BURTON

Giving Blood

I need money for the taxi cab ride home to the
    reservation and
I need a taxi
because all the Indians left this city last night while I was
    sleeping
and forgot to tell me
so I walk on down to the blood bank with a coupon that
    guarantees
me twenty bucks a pint
and I figure I can stand to lose three or four pints but the
white nurse says no
you can only give up one pint at a time and before you
    can do that
you have to clear
our extensive screening process which involves a physical
    examination
and interview
which is a pain in the ass but I need the money so I sit
    down
at a wooden desk
across from the white nurse holding a pen and paper and
    she asks me
my name and I tell her
Crazy Horse and she asks my birthdate and I tell her it
    was probably
June 25 in 1876 and then she asks my ethnic origin and I
    tell her I'm an

Indian or Native American
depending on your view of historical accuracy and she
    asks me
my religious preference and I tell her I prefer to keep my
    religion entirely independent
of my economic activities
and then she asks me how many sexual partners I've
    had and
I say one or two
depending on your definition of what I did to Custer
    and then
she puts aside her pen and paper
and gives me the most important question she asks me
if I still have enough heart
and I tell her I don't know it's been a long time but I'd
    like to
give it a try
and then she smiles and turns to her computer punches
    in my name
and vital information
and we wait together for the results until the computer
    prints
a sheet of statistics
and the white nurse reads it over a few times and tells
    me I'm
sorry Mr. Crazy Horse
but we've already taken too much of your blood and you
    won't be eligible
to donate for another generation or two

SHERMAN ALEXIE

The Body of Man

The body of man is like a flicker of lightning
existing only to return to Nothingness.
Like the spring growth that shrivels in autumn.
Waste no thought on the process for it has no purpose,
coming and going like the dew.

VAN HANH

*(Translated from the Vietnamese by Nguyen Ngoc Bich with
W. S. Merwin)*

Scleroderma at Fifteen

Of course there were things I didn't like,
Though it wasn't really bad.
But then the doctors told me 'bout a problem that I have.
They did a lot of funny tests and poked and prodded me.
It now seems I'm not as healthy as I might appear to be.
My body's turning on itself; it seems to want me dead,
Like the bitter voice that sneers at all my actions in
    my head.
My body creaks and shrieks at me.
My hands smart in the cold;
The mist seeps deep into my bones, making me feel old.
And so I eat up little pearls they say will help me win.
They make my body yelp, they make my senses sneeze
    and swim.
I don't know how to fight this war where there's no her
    or him.
But there's still hope that's floating here,
An ever-glowing spark.
I just don't know who to talk to.
And I can't sleep when it is dark.

ERIN JOHNSON

Dem Dry Bones

Ezekiel connected dem dry bones
Ezekiel connected dem dry bones
Ezekiel connected dem dry bones
I hear the word of the Lord.

Your toe bone connected to your foot bone,
Your foot bone connected to your ankle bone,
Your ankle bone connected to your leg bone,
Your leg bone connected to your knee bone,
Your knee bone connected to your thigh bone,
Your thigh bone connected to your hip bone,
Your hip bone connected to your back bone,
Your back bone connected to your shoulder bone,
Your shoulder bone connected to your neck bone,
Your neck bone connected to your head bone,
I hear the word of the Lord!

Dem bones, dem bones, gonna walk aroun'
Dem bones, dem bones, gonna walk aroun'
Dem bones, dem bones, gonna walk aroun'
I hear the word of the Lord!

Disconnect dem bones, dem dry bones
Disconnect dem bones, dem dry bones
Disconnect dem bones, dem dry bones
I hear the word of the Lord!

Your head bone connected from your neck bone,
Your neck bone connected from your shoulder bone,

Your shoulder bone connected from your back bone,
Your back bone connected from your hip bone,
Your hip bone connected from your thigh bone,
Your thigh bone connected from your knee bone,
Your knee bone connected from your leg bone,
Your leg bone connected from your ankle bone,
Your ankle bone connected from your foot bone,
Your foot bone connected from your toe bone,
I hear the word of the Lord!
I hear the word of the Lord!

ANONYMOUS

Breath

I remember coming up,
pushing off from the bottom
through dull ringing silence
toward the undersurface of the water
where light sparkled—or patterns
fanned across the roof-fabric:
that deep comfort, long ago, of
being carried to the house
in the dark, half-asleep, only
half-interrupting the dreams
that had made the car a craft
among stars. But the air—
and the house—held
depths too, where someone else,
someone larger, locked the doors, did
late-night chores and turned out
the lights, too tired now
to stop the inevitable
fight, rising to it . . .

Underwater, you hear bodies
burble over you, smashing the sunlight—
and voices in other rooms begin
to swell, drawers shutting, bags
slammed down from the closet shelves,
footsteps . . . Till a child's fear,
held under, shudders free, floating up
to explode with a gasp, and splashes

out of sleep, and sucks air,
and discovers that nothing
consoles, there is no air,
there is no waking, not anywhere.

REGINALD GIBBONS

Flipped on Its Axis,
from Listen to Our Voices

ALTERNATE TEENAGE VOICES: When he hits me. When she hits me. When I get hit. When he hits my mother.

LUIS: When he hit me, it used to hurt. I mean, I was shocked at how much his fists could hurt. It took me a second to realize this man, my father, was punching me. I didn't know what to do. I was so much smaller than he was. I kind of put my hands up, tried to block his hands, his big hands. It didn't do much good. It was like he wanted to punch me right into the ground, into the universe, make me disappear. God, how I wished I could.

CHRISTOPHER: Shock is the thing you have to deal with. It would be different if you got a beating at school by a guy or something. Like you know you did something wrong and then got into trouble. That's bad enough. But your (ALTERNATE VOICES: *father/ stepfather/ mother/ boyfriend/ stepmother*)! That's when everything starts to fall apart. You're supposed to have loyalty or something for them. They're supposed to take care of you. Everything I've ever learned outside of the home—on television, in books, in stories— parents are supposed to take of care of their young. What happens to you when you find out you didn't get that kind of parents?

LUIS: You spend a lot of time alone at first. It's sort of like you've got to settle it in your head, except it never settles. You don't want to tell anyone. You try to cover up the marks. You feel somewhere in your body that you are going to be a man too, but when he beats you, you feel like such a little boy. Everything gets flipped on its axis.

ERIN: No one ever hit me. Maybe a spanking when I was a kid, but nothing like the other kids. It wouldn't have done any good anyway. It would have just made things worse. I was bad enough without them adding to it. Beating a kid never made a bad kid good. I don't know if anything can ever make me good. I don't know what good is, and that's the truth.

CHRYSTAL: Everything you thought was true isn't true anymore. You aren't safe. Your own home is enemy territory. You are supposed to love the enemy. You have no one. You wish you weren't born.

AMBER: Then instead of things getting better, they get worse.

LUIS: You can't defend yourself. The anger gets worse.

CHRISTOPHER: It goes inside. You can't live in fear and rage without something happening.

AMBER: It doesn't work that way. First the grades all go to hell.

CHRYSTAL: Then you start the downhill road that leads you into juvenile hall. Then you're locked up.

LUIS: Then you're away from him, at least for a while. But the worst thing is that his blood runs in my veins. I think about it a lot. His blood and rage and him. I guess that's why I'm violent.

SYLVIA: He told me that he loved me and that's what caused him to do it. To me it looked like jealousy, not love. I want to cry but I won't. Then he slaps me, pinches me. It started with the verbal stuff—"slut," "whore"—then it got physical. I wrote him a letter, said I didn't want to see him again. I haven't gotten up the nerve to send it.

(ALTERNATE VOICES *again*): When he beats me, I beat someone else. I feel like garbage sometimes. I've become everything he said I would. I'm a menace to society. I'm every parent's nightmare. It's too late for me. He beat every hope I ever had into a pulp. To look at me you'd never know, would you? I could have been a regular kid, just like you. I could have been happy. Now when people here at Redwoods ask me to say one nice thing about myself I just sit there and look at them. Can't they see there is nothing good to say?

AMBER: When he hits my mother it's as if I'm in a horror movie and can't get out. I can't block the sound and the agony. I want to kill him. I want to kill myself sometimes. I want this nightmare to stop. Sometimes it's like a horror movie. There's a monster in my house. I call him my father.

CHRYSTAL: You try to just pretend that everything is normal. Then when you try to go to sleep at night, memories come back. It's like your body remembers even when your mind tries to forget. It's hard growing up. Your body takes on so many changes. Sometimes you're not ready for it. You're just a kid and then all of a sudden, things begin happening to you. Whether you're ready or not. Then people start looking at you differently. You're becoming a woman, and inside there's still this little-girl mind. You know, sometimes I look back to when I was young, and I think, God how stupid we are as kids. We're so simple. We trust everyone. We think people love us. Before . . . before it happened I was a normal kid. I have a hard time around guys now. I'm afraid to be alone with them. I'm afraid to go out alone. I know all guys are not like him. I don't like my body much. I think of places he touched and I hate those places. It's like I can't wash it away. They haven't made that kind of soap yet. My body scares me. Everything sçares me. Then I lash out. Then I started what everyone called acting out. I mean he only got a few months in jail. Not enough evidence. He could be looking for me now. Who knows? I'm scared to be out at night. I cry a lot. I was raped.

CLAIRE BRAZ-VALENTINE

no parts spared
for Sabaah

woke up today
surprised myself
stray bullets poppin' inside me
like radiated icicles
dreamin' this was
The Day
body would finally
loosen up enough so real me
could go on about my business
flesh and bones holdin' on with a python's clutch
like i ain't got stuff to do
without being weighed down
in this 100 pound cemented suit
lead bound feet
hands dipped in acid rain
naw this ain't no travelin' boat i'm in
a war hit ship
hazard waste infested
pesticide injected
my spirit struggles against a spiked iron lung
belly full of molten crabs
and a pack of rabid dogs scratchin' my throat
so it's nearin'
grim reaper's scythe hovers overhead
gonna whip me away
and i ain't scared no mo'
pain finally beat up fear in the battle of the fittest
pistol whipped triple overtime
just a matter of a few more notes plucked

from rotted janglin' teeth
before i get to tie on my travelin' shoes
so for now
i lay here payin' homage to volcanoes
formin' on my thighs
bile leakin' out my ears
hair like wintered leaves
though it hurts to blink
i click my lids diggin' the sounds of rusted plates
though motion opens
howlin' gates
i slow rock conjurin' up the wolf's cackle
i keep my nose tilted
but still quicksand spurts out
coverin' snot stained sheets with rancid goop
my greatest feat is turnin' pain into a game
i'm in costume when i see
worms diggin' through my face
markin' territory with tar 'n' feces
bald is trendy as bone protrudes through fish skin
0% body fat is the American Dream
in between there's the wind rushin' thru to disembowel
make me fess up to crimes i ain't committed
i withstand the call to walk on clouds
bludgeon myself with a hatchet
or put my name on Kevorkian's things to do list
now when glass travels through my veins
i give laughter new names
i tally time on my bed post
with the venom that oozes out my pores
acceptin' vice's grip with arms wide open
makin' games out of pain

comparin' it to pleasure
FACT: i have moaned the exact same sounds
when i've had ecstasy swirl inside me
as i now do
engulfed by stagnant cesspools of fermented mud
acceptance is pure
purity is uncontaminated
and because i have accepted my body rottin'
before my eyes
I have become well . . . wholesome . . . regenerated
and now that I've become whole again in spite of
my insides clawin' me to extinction
I concentrate more on the livin'
I hear pain from calloused hearts whose owners
disown razor embedded memories
(forgettin' is akin to blunted realities)
souls like these reach out for me now
wounded plexus findin' comfort in the born again
I place my ear against scabs
listen to blood
I stroke the stuff folks blind themselves to
whisper lullabies to matted yarns
watch the ungnarlin'
stroke as ulcerated cores
become clear again
whisper lullabies
healin' begins
I stroke   whisper

The Healin' Begins

TISH BENSON

Still Life

The bullet has almost entered the brain:
I can feel it sprint down the gun barrel,
rolling each bevel around like a hoop
on a pigslide of calibrated steel and oil.
Now it whistles free and aloft
in that ice-cold millimeter of air,
then boils as the first layer of skin
shales off like ragged leaves of soap.
The trigger's omnipresent click
makes triggers all over the body fire.
Now it tunnels through palisades,
veins, arteries, white corpuscles
red and battered as swollen ghosts,
cuts the struts on a glacial bone
jutting out like the leg of a single flamingo,
feints and draws in close for the kill,
egged on by a mouse-gray parliament of cells.

DIANE ACKERMAN

Thinking About Bill, Dead of AIDS

We did not know the first thing about
how blood surrenders to even the smallest threat
when old allergies turn inside out,

the body rescinding all its normal orders
to all defenders of flesh, betraying the head,
pulling its guards back from all its borders.

Thinking of friends afraid to shake your hand,
we think of your hand shaking, your mouth set,
your eyes drained of any reprimand.

Loving, we kissed you, partly to persuade
both you and us, seeing what eyes had said,
that we were loving and were not afraid.

If we had had more, we would have given more.
As it was we stood next to your bed,
stopping, though, to set our smiles at the door.

Not because we were less sure at the last.
Only because, not knowing anything yet,
we didn't know what look would hurt you least.

MILLER WILLIAMS

S M

I tell you, Chickadee
I am afraid of people
who cannot cry
Tears left unshed
turn to poison
in the ducts
Ask the next soldier you see
enjoying a massacre
if this is not so.

People who do not cry
are victims
of soul mutilation
paid for in Marlboros
and trucks.

Resist.

Violence does not work
except for the man
who pays your salary
Who knows
if you could still weep
you would not take the job.

ALICE WALKER

The Cutting Edge

At thirteen, I begin cutting myself; an accident, really, that first cut. Bored and lonely, nothing to do on a late August afternoon. My best friend is away at camp for two weeks; the severe summer's heat threatens to ignite me.

Sitting on the back-porch steps, my Girl Scout knife open. I'd been playing darts with it for a while, throwing the knife down into a circular dartboard drawn in the backyard dirt patch. Tired of this solitary game, I begin making imaginary tattoos by pulling the knife's blade across my freckled forearm. The blade forms a series of flaky, white scratches on my skin until I push the blade in too deeply. Then a small band of pink gradually turns red. I have cut myself but feel no pain. Intrigued by this, I purposefully cut myself a second time, a slightly larger, deeper cut. I like this flood of electricity that surges through my body, a sweet rush.

Soon, each day I play this new game with my knife. At night I slip into my closet, sit down on the worn wood floor and cut myself, up high on my thigh or on my butt. The shadowy closet no longer frightens me as it did when I was a child. I lean back into my clothes, feel worn denim or wool scratch my face as I take my time putting on a Band-Aid stolen from the bathroom cabinet. Cutting has become a daily event only I am allowed to participate in.

When school starts again, I walk into homeroom each day feeling the soft soreness of a fresh cut rub against the elastic band of underwear, that soft glove of dull pain holds me as I sit down at my desk. I run my fingers over the aged wooden desktop and smile as I read years of bored students' cuts and gashes—"M.T. & E.C. 4ever"; "Stacy luvs Bill"; "Wilson SUCKS!"; "Go Redskins!"

I look at other girls as they walk into the room, knowing I do not belong with them. I am not popular or athletic, the brainiest or the prettiest. Also, because my family has once again moved into a new town, I am again the new girl in school, invisible. I've changed schools three times in the past two years. Each move leaves me feeling more fragmented, a piece of me left behind in each town. My secret ceremony, cutting, is something I carry from move to move. My toughness, my lack of queasiness or timidity puts me into an elite category. When I hurt myself, I do not cry.

Razor blades soon replace the Girl Scout knife. The first blade of thin gleaming aluminum is stolen from Dad's pack of razors. I don't want to be found out so I use allowance money to buy my own razors, Band-Aids, and a large jar of Vaseline, needed to stop blood from dripping onto the closet floor. The razor cuts make fine, hairline slashes on my arms and legs, which, when my skin tans, remain white and remind me of tiny fish-bone tracks.

Two months into the new school year, I no longer bother to hide my cuts. If asked, I explain them away easily enough as cat scratches, tree-branch scrapes. By now I am addicted to the adrenaline rush each cut brings. I crave this brief sensation, rely on it especially when life threatens to pull me down.

After each cut, I become light-headed, give way to nervous, edgy giggles. My body so light, I am convinced that if I stand up and hold out my arms, I will float away from everyone, everything, like a helium balloon, untroubled, free.

BARBARA HILL

My Tattoo

I thought I wanted to wear
the Sacred Heart, to represent
education through suffering,

how we're pierced to flame.
But when I cruised
the inkshop's dragons,

cobalt tigers and eagles
in billowy smokes,
my allegiance wavered.

Butch lexicon,
anchors and arrows,
a sailor's iconic charms—

tempting, but none
of them me. What noun
would you want

spoken on your skin
your whole life through?
I tried to picture what

I'd never want erased,
and saw a fire-ring corona
of spiked rays,

flaring tongues
surrounding—an emptiness,
an open space?

I made my mind up.
I sat in the waiting room chair.
Then something (my nerve?

faith in the guy
with biker boots
and indigo hands?)

wavered. It wasn't fear;
nothing hurts like grief,
and I'm used to that.

His dreaming needle
was beside the point;
don't I already bear

the etched and flaring marks
of an inky trade?
What once was skin

has turned to something
made; written and revised
beneath these sleeves:

hearts and banners,
daggers and flowers and names.
I fled. Then I came back again;

isn't there always
a little more room
on the skin? It's too late

to be unwritten,
and I'm much too scrawled
to ever be erased.

Go ahead: prick and stipple
and ink me in:
I'll never be naked again.

From here on out,
I wear the sun,
albeit blue.

MARK DOTY

From The Woodlanders

The young woman laid down the bill-hook for a moment and examined the palm of her right hand which, unlike the other, was ungloved, and showed little hardness or roughness about it. The palm was red and blistering, as if her present occupation were as yet too recent to have subdued it to what it worked in. As with so many right hands born to manual labour, there was nothing in its fundamental shape to bear out the physiological conventionalism that gradations of birth show themselves primarily in the form of this member. Nothing but a cast of the die of destiny had decided that the girl should handle the tool; and the fingers which clasped the heavy ash haft might have skilfully guided the pencil or swept the string, had they only been set to do it in good time.

Her face had the usual fulness of expression which is developed by a life of solitude. Where the eyes of a multitude continuously beat like waves upon a countenance they seem to wear away its mobile power; but in the still water of privacy every feeling and sentiment unfolds in visible luxuriance, to be interpreted as readily as a printed word by an intruder. In years she was no more than nineteen or twenty, but the necessity of taking thought at a too early period of life had forced the provisional curves of her childhood's face to a premature finality. Thus she had but little pretension to beauty, save in one prominent particular—her hair.

Its abundance made it almost unmanageable; its colour was, roughly speaking, and as seen here by firelight, brown; but careful notice, or an observation by day, would have revealed that its true shade was a rare and beautiful approximation to chestnut.

On this one bright gift of Time to the particular victim of his now before us the newcomer's eyes were fixed; meanwhile the fingers of his right hand mechanically played over something sticking up from his waistcoat pocket—the bows of a pair of scissors, whose polish made them feebly responsive to the light from within the house. In her present beholder's mind the scene formed by the girlish spar-maker composed itself into an impression-picture of extremest type, wherein the girl's hair alone, as the focus of observation, was depicted with intensity and distinctness, while her face, shoulders, hands, and figure in general were a blurred mass of unimportant detail lost in haze and obscurity.

He hesitated no longer, but tapped at the door and entered. The young woman turned at the crunch of his boots on the sanded floor, and exclaiming, 'O, Mr Percomb, how you frightened me!' quite lost her colour for a moment.

He replied, 'You should shut your door—then you'd hear folk open it.'

'I can't,' she said; 'the chimney smokes so. Mr Percomb, you look as unnatural away from your wigs as a canary in a thorn hedge. Surely you have not come out here on my account—for—'

'Yes—to have your answer about this.' He touched her hair with his cane, and she winced. 'Do you agree?' he continued. 'It is necessary that I should know at once, as the lady is soon going away, and it takes time to make up.'

'Don't press me—it worries me. I was in hopes you had thought no more of it. I can *not* part with it—so there!'

'Now look here, Marty,' said the other, sitting down on the coffin-stool table. 'How much do you get for making these spars?'

'Hush—father's upstairs awake, and he don't know that I am doing his work.'

'Well, now tell me,' said the man more softly. 'How much do you get?'

'Eighteenpence a thousand,' she said reluctantly.

'Who are you making them for?'

'Mr Melbury, the timber-dealer, just below here.'

'And how many can you make in a day?'

'In a day and half the night, three bundles—that's a thousand and a half.'

'Two and threepence.' Her visitor paused. 'Well, look here,' he continued with the remains of a computation in his tone, which reckoning had been to fix the probable sum of money necessary to outweigh her present resources and her woman's love of comeliness; 'here's a sovereign—a gold sovereign, almost new.' He held it out between his finger and thumb. 'That's as much as you'd earn in a week and a half at that rough man's-work, and it's yours for just letting me snip off what you've got too much of.'

The girl's bosom moved a very little. 'Why can't the lady send to some other girl who don't value her hair—not to me?' she exclaimed.

'Why, simpleton, because yours is the exact shade of her own, and 'tis a shade you can't match by dyeing. But you are not going to refuse me now I've come all the way from Sherton on purpose?'

'I say I won't sell it—to you or anybody.'

'Now listen,' and he drew up a little closer beside her. 'The lady is very rich, and won't be particular to a few shillings; so I will advance to this on my own responsibility—I'll make the one sovereign two, rather than go back empty-handed.'

'No, no, no!' she cried, beginning to be much agitated. 'You are tempting me. You go on like the Devil to Doctor Faustus in the penny book. But I don't want your money, and won't agree. Why did you come? I said when you got me into your shop and urged me so much that I didn't mean to sell my hair!'

'Marty, now hearken. The lady that wants it wants it badly. And, between you and me, you'd better let her have it. 'Twill be bad for you if you don't.'

'Bad for me? Who is she, then?'

The wig-maker held his tongue, and the girl repeated the question.

'I am not at liberty to tell you. And as she is going abroad soon it makes no difference who she is at all.'

'She wants it to go abroad wi'?'

He assented by a nod.

The girl regarded him reflectively. 'Now, Mr Percomb,' she said, 'I know who 'tis. 'Tis she at the House—Mrs Charmond!'

'That's my secret. However, if you agree to let me have it I'll tell you in confidence.'

'I'll certainly not let you have it unless you tell me the truth. Is it Mrs Charmond?'

The man dropped his voice. 'Well—it is. You sat in front of her in church the other day, and she noticed how exactly your hair matches her own. Ever since then she's been hankering for it, to help out hers, and at last decided to get it. As she won't wear it till she goes off abroad she knows nobody will recognize the change. I'm commissioned to get it for her, and then it is to be made up. I shouldn't have vamped all these miles for any less important employer. Now, mind—'tis as much as my business with her is worth if it should be known that I've let out her name; but honour between us two, Marty, and you'll say nothing that would injure me?'

'I don't wish to tell upon her,' said Marty coolly. 'But my hair is my own, and I'm going to keep it.'

'Now that's not fair, after what I've told you,' said the nettled emissary. 'You see, Marty, as you are in the same parish, and in one of this lady's cottages, and your father is ill, and wouldn't like to turn out, it would be as well to oblige her. I say that as a friend. But I won't press you to make up your mind to-night. You'll be coming to market to-morrow, I dare say, and you can call then. If you think it over you'll be inclined to bring what I want, I know.'

'I've nothing more to say,' she answered.

Her companion saw from her manner that it was useless to urge her further by speech. 'As you are a trusty young woman,' he said, 'I'll put these sovereigns up here for ornament, that you may see how handsome they are. Bring the article to-morrow, or return the sovereigns.' He stuck them edgewise into the frame of a small mantel looking-glass. 'I hope you'll bring it; for your sake and mine. I should have thought she could have suited herself elsewhere; but as it's her fancy it must be indulged if possible. If you cut it off yourself, mind how you do it so as to keep all the locks one way.' He showed her how this was to be done.

'But I shan't,' she replied with laconic indifference. 'I value my looks too much to spoil 'em. She wants my curls to get another lover with; though if stories are true she's broke the heart of many a noble gentleman already.'

'Lord, it's wonderful how you guess things, Marty,' said the barber. 'I've had it from those that know that there certainly is some foreign gentleman in her eye. However, mind what I ask.'

'She's not going to get him through me.'

Percomb had retired as far as the door; he came back, planted his cane on the coffin-stool, and looked her in the face. 'Marty South,' he said with deliberate emphasis, *you've got a lover yourself,* and that's why you won't let it go!'

She reddened so intensely as to pass the mild blush that suffices to heighten beauty; she put the yellow leather glove on one hand, took up the hook with the other, and sat down doggedly to her work without turning her face to him again. He regarded her head for a moment, went to the door, and with one look back at her departed on his way homeward.

Marty pursued her occupation for a few minutes, then suddenly laying down the bill-hook she jumped up and went to the back of the room, where she opened a door which disclosed a staircase so whitely scrubbed that the grain of the wood was well-nigh sodden away by cleansing. At the top she gently approached a bedroom, and without entering said, 'Father, do you want anything?'

A weak voice inside answered in the negative; adding, 'I should be all right by to-morrow if it were not for the tree!'

'The tree again—always the tree! O, father, don't worry so about that. You know it can do you no harm.'

'Who have ye had talking to 'ee downstairs?'

'A Sherton man called—nothing to trouble about,' she said soothingly. 'Father,' she went on, 'can Mrs Charmond turn us out of our house if she's minded to?'

'Turn us out? No. Nobody can turn us out till my poor soul is turned out of my body. 'Tis lifehold, like Giles Winterborne's. But when my life drops 'twill be hers—not till then.' His words on this subject so far had been rational and firm enough. But now he lapsed into his moaning strain: 'And the tree will do it—that tree will soon be the death of me.'

'Nonsense, you know better. How can it be?' She refrained from further speech, and descended to the ground floor again.

'Thank Heaven then,' she said to herself, 'what belongs to me I keep.'

THOMAS HARDY

Hot Combs

At the junk shop, I find an old pair,
black with grease, the teeth still pungent
as burning hair. One is small,
fine toothed as if for a child. Holding it,
I think of my mother's slender wrist,
the curve of her neck as she leaned
over the stove, her eyes shut as she pulled
the wooden handle and laid flat the wisps
at her temples. The heat in our kitchen
made her glow that morning. I watched her
wincing, the hot comb singeing her brow,
sweat glistening above her lips,
her face made strangely beautiful
as only suffering can do.

NATASHA TRETHEWEY

Pimples

They always come in groups:
odd, un-symmetrical,
un-choreographed gibberish.

On the lower left corner of my chin,
behind my ears, between my eyes,
those deformed triangular blemishes.

And I hate it when my pimples
resemble constellations,
concentrated in league
on the bacteria-infested areas
of my adolescent epidermis.

"Get yourself some Clearasil,"
someone once told me,
yet my situation is genetic:
I cannot help being
the poster boy for brand-x.
You see I'm pizza face,
with extra toppings.

I only wish you would look
beyond my pimples,
and kiss me for who I am inside.

ANDREW NIELSEN

Unscratchable Itch

There is a spot that you can't scratch
Right between your shoulder blades,
Like an egg that just won't hatch
Here you set and there it stays.
Turn and squirm and try to reach it,
Twist your neck and bend your back,
Hear your elbows creak and crack,
Stretch your fingers, now you bet it's
Going to reach—no that won't get it—
Hold your breath and stretch and pray,
Only just an inch away,
Worse than a sunbeam you can't catch
Is that one spot that
You can't scratch.

SHEL SILVERSTEIN

Blinking

You've got to love life so much that you don't want to miss a moment of it, and pay such close attention to whatever you're doing that each time you blink you can hear your eyelashes applauding what you've just seen.

In each eye there are more than 80 eyelashes, forty above and forty below, like forty pairs of arms working, 80 pairs in both eyes, a whole audience clapping so loud you can hardly bear to listen.

160 hands batter each other every time you blink. "Bravo!" they call. "Encore! Encore!"

Paralyzed in a hospital bed, or watching the cold rain from under a bridge—remember this.

MORTON MARCUS

The Runner

On a flat road runs the well-train'd runner,
He is lean and sinewy with muscular legs,
He is thinly clothed, he leans forward as he runs,
With lightly closed fists and arms partially rais'd.

WALT WHITMAN

Swimmers

Tossed
by the muscular sea,
we are lost,
and glad to be lost
in troughs of rough

love. A bath in
laughter, our dive
into foam,
our upslide and float
on the surf of desire.

But sucked to the root
of the water-mountain—
immense—
about to tip upon us
the terror of total

delight—
we are towed,
helpless in its
swell, by hooks
of our hair;

then dangled, let go,
made to race—
as the wrestling chest
of the sea, itself
tangled, tumbles

in its own embrace.
Our limbs like eels
are water-boned,
our faces lost
to difference and

contour, as the lapping
crests.
They cease
their charge,
and rock us

in repeating hammocks
of the releasing
tide—
until supine we glide,
on cool green

smiles
of an exhaling
gladiator,
to the shore
of sleep.

MAY SWENSON

When I Arise Glistening

In the shower,
my song can burst forth
for I feel safe
    where groomed by liquid phalanxes.

I stop,
and breathe
while enveloped in water
    enclosed in my tub
        set in my bathroom
            deep in my apartment,
                I'm in the womb of my home.

I feel my body's temperature rise
    to meet that of the water's
    as I reach for my soap
    my brush
    my implements of deconstruction are needed
            though I have already consented to
            washing my shit down the drain.

I need the water
as it kneads me,
    loosening my tense head, shoulders, neck . . .

I come to consciousness
grasping my showerhead microphone,
it as wet with my spray as I with its.

And I realize I have forgotten
    the world outside my curtain.

So,
    relaxing my chest,
    expanding
    contracting my diaphragm,
    breathing as easy as a melody . . .

        I can feel it moving
        on the altar of my heart
        every now and then.

And when I arise glistening from the shower,
I am always surprised by the clean
bronze woman I see in the mirror.
She stands proud and naked before me.
Only she expected,
demanded even,
the peace-filled eyes
that return her bold gaze.

DEBORAH TURNER

A Hindu to His Body

Dear pursuing presence,
dear body: you brought me
curled in womb and memory.

Gave me fingers to clutch
at grace, at malice; and ruffle
someone else's hair; to fold a man's
shadow back on his world;
to hold in the dark of the eye
through a winter and a fear
the poise, the shape of a breast;
a pear's silence, in the calyx
and the noise of a childish fist.

You brought me: do not leave me
behind. When you leave all else,
my garrulous face, my unkissed
alien mind, when you muffle
and put away my pulse
to rise in the sap of trees
let me go with you and feel the weight
of honey-hives in my branching
and the burlap weave of weaver-birds
in my hair.

A. K. RAMANUJAN

To Sleep

Come, Sleep, O Sleep, the certain knot of peace,
　　The baiting-place of wit, the balm of woe,
The poor man's wealth, the prisoner's release,
　　The indifferent judge between the high and low;
With shield of proof shield me from out the press
　　Of those fierce darts Despair at me doth throw:
O make in me those civil wars to cease;
　　I will good tribute pay, if thou do so.
Take thou of me smooth pillows, sweetest bed,
　　A chamber deaf to noise and blind to light,
A rosy garland and a weary head;
　　And if these things, as being thine by right,
　　　　Move not thy heavy grace, thou shalt in me,
　　　　Livelier than elsewhere, Stella's image see.

SIR PHILIP SIDNEY

"He wheeled a corpse"

He wheeled a corpse into the narrow furnace, and said, there's something I want to show you. He lit the gas, and the head rose from the table, the arms flew away from the bones, and the bones snapped and burned with a fierce blue flame. When the oven had cooled and the door was opened, the ashes and bits of bone threw off a pale, opalescent light. That light, he said, is what I wanted you to see.

GARY YOUNG

Legacy

my face is grass
          color of April rain;
arms, legs are the limbs
          of birch, cedar;
my thoughts are winds
          which blow;
pictures in my mind
                    are the climb up hill
                    to dream in the sun;
                    hawk feathers, and quills
                    of porcupine running
                    the edge of the stream
                    which reflects stories
                    of my many mornings
                    and the dark faces of night
                    mingled with victories
                    of dawn and tomorrow;
corn of the fields and squash . . .
                    the daughters of my mother
                    who collect honey
                    and all the fruits;
meadow and sky are the end of my day,
                    the stretch of my night
                    yet the birth of my dust;
my wind is the breath of a fawn
                    the cry of the cub
                    the trot of the wolf
                    whose print covers
                    the tracks of my feet;

my word, my word,
            loaned
legacy, the obligation I hand
            to the blood of my flesh
            and the sinew of the loins
to hold to the sun
            and the moon
which direct the river
            that carries my song
            and the beat of the drum
to the fires of the village
            which endures.

MAURICE KENNY

Biographical Notes

The quotes contained within the biographies below are from interviews, letters, or readily available sources, such as the World Wide Web.

Poet and writer **DIANE ACKERMAN** (b. 1948) was born in Illinois. She received an M.A., M.F.A., and Ph.D. from Cornell University. Ackerman lives in Ithaca, New York, with her husband, the writer Paul West. She has taught at several universities. Her book *Jaguar of Sweet Laughter: New and Selected Poems* was named a Notable Book of the Year in 1991 by the *New York Times Book Review*.

Ackerman says, "If I had my druthers, every prose book I wrote would be like inhaling jungle. It would all be at a level of poetic intensity that I would find satisfying word by word. Sentence by sentence. Page by page. But, unfortunately, I've discovered that books have to have transitions. The sun can't always be at noon, and there are times when you actually have to explain yourself. Or you have to move people around in the landscape and stuff like that. But I have a poet's heart and a poet's sensibility."

SUGGESTED READING
Jaguar of Sweet Laughter: New and Selected Poems (Vintage Books)
The Moon by Whale Light: And Other Adventures Among Bats, Penguins, Crocodilians, and Whales (nonfiction; Vintage Books)
A Natural History of the Senses (nonfiction; Vintage Books)

FRANCISCO X. ALARCÓN (b. 1954), Chicano poet and educator, was born in Los Angeles, California, and grew up in Guadalajara, Mexico. He is the author of 10 volumes of poetry and several bilingual books for children. Two of his children's books won the Pura Belpré Honor Award from the American Library Association. Alarcón did his undergraduate studies at California State University, Long Beach, and his graduate work at Stanford University. He currently teaches at the University of California, Davis, where he directs the Spanish for Native Speakers Program.

Alarcón writes, "My poem titled 'Bridge' first appeared in a collective book of poems I published in San Francisco in 1985 with two other Chicano friends of mine, Juan Pablo Gutiérrez and Rodrigo Reyes. The book, *Ya vas, carnal,* which could be translated as 'All right, brother,' is probably the first homoerotic collection of poems published by Latino gay males in the United States. I wrote 'Bridge' as a celebration of the love of a man towards another man. I believe that by loving and touching our lover's body, we are able to save ourselves. For me, love and sex are true expressions of what is sacred in all of us.

"'I Used to Be Much Much Darker' is also an autobiographical poem. After spending a few months at Stanford University studying as a graduate student, I went home to visit my family in Southern California. Upon seeing me, Mother asked me what had happened to me since I had lost my dark-color complexion. I was really taken by her question, and noticed that, in fact, I was not as 'dark' as I used to be. I wrote this poem as a response. When I read my poem aloud, many people usually laugh at the beginning but are a bit disturbed by the last lines 'up here "dark" / is only for / the ashes / the stuff / lonely nights / are made of.' The key to this poem is the word 'dark' that can have many different and sometimes contradictory meanings."

SUGGESTED READING

Body in Flames / Cuerpo en llamas (poems; Chronicle Books)
Snake Poems: An Aztec Invocation (Chronicle Books)
Sonnets to Madness and Other Misfortunes / Sonetos a la locura y otras penas (Creative Arts Book Company)
Angels Ride Bikes and Other Fall Poems (Children's Book Press)
Iguanas in the Snow and Other Winter Poems (Children's Book Press)

Native-American poet and novelist SHERMAN ALEXIE (b. 1966) had a difficult start in life. Born hydrocephalic, he survived brain surgery when he was six months old, but wasn't expected to live. Not only did he survive, but he also disproved doctors' predictions that he would be mentally retarded, and has become an internationally known and highly acclaimed writer.

Alexie says he began writing because he "kept fainting in anatomy class and needed a career change. The only class that fit where the human anatomy class had been was a poetry writing workshop." His first book of poetry, *The Business of Fancydancing*, which garnered Alexie great reviews, was published when he was 25. Alexie's first screenplay was based on his book *The Lone Ranger and Tonto Fistfight in Heaven*. It was the first feature film that was produced, written, and directed by Native Americans. About his literary influences, Alexie says, "Walt Whitman and Emily Dickinson are two of my favorites. I always tell people my literary influences are Stephen King, John Steinbeck, and my mother, and my grandfather, and the Brady Bunch."

SUGGESTED READING

The Business of Fancydancing: Stories and Poems (Hanging Loose Press)

Reservation Blues (novel; Warner Books)
The Lone Ranger and Tonto Fistfight in Heaven (short stories; HarperPerennial)
The Toughest Indian in the World (short stories; Grove Press)

ANONYMOUS—"Dem Dry Bones," also known as "Dem Bones" and "Dry Bones," is a well-known and well-loved African-American spiritual. The song is about resurrection, based on the biblical prophet Ezekiel's vision. He saw "a great many bones on the floor of the valley, bones that were very dry." Then the bones joined together at God's command, but there was no breath in them until God breathed upon them and they came to life again. The ringing narrative of this song, the use of repetition, compels listeners and singers—it is difficult to listen and not sing. It was probably first sung in church and at revival meetings two hundred years ago. Like other songs and poems that were learned first by heart and passed down by word of mouth, this one has many versions.

SUGGESTED READING
All Night, All Day: A Child's First Book of African-American Spirituals (selected and illustrated by Ashley Bryan; Atheneum)
I'm Going to Sing: Black American Spirituals (selected and illustrated by Ashley Bryan; Atheneum)
My Songs: Aframerican Religious Folk Songs (arranged and interpreted by Roland Hayes; Little, Brown & Co.)

ELLEN BASS (b. 1947) grew up in New Jersey, received an M.A. in creative writing from Boston University, and has taught creative writing for more than 25 years. She began writing poetry in junior high school as an outlet for troubled feelings and has been writing ever since. Her awards include the Elliston Book Award and *Nimrod*/Hardman's Pablo Neruda Prize for Poetry. Bass lives with her partner, Janet, with whom she's raised two children in Santa Cruz, California.

Bass writes, "'They Lied' was inspired by one of my students who had been so abused and criticized as a child that she lost her ability to know her own being—body and soul— as beautiful. Poetry, for me, is a way to say what can't be said—or truly heard—in conversation.

"I was a little nervous when I shared this poem with the woman to whom it's addressed. I hoped she wouldn't be offended by the intimacy or the liberties I'd taken. I was gratified when she received it as the honoring I'd intended."

SUGGESTED READING
Everything on the Menu (poems; BOA Editions, Ltd.)

ERIN BELIEU (b. 1956) was born in Omaha, Nebraska, and educated at the University of Nebraska, Ohio State University, and Boston University. In addition to winning the National Poetry Series, she has received the Academy of American Poets Prize.

SUGGESTED READING
Infanta (poems; Copper Canyon Press)
One Above & One Below (poems; Copper Canyon Press)
The Extraordinary Tide: New Poetry by American Women (anthology; Columbia University Press)

TISH BENSON (b. 1966), a Texas-born writer and performer, currently lives in Brooklyn. She graduated with an M.F.A. in dramatic writing from New York University, and she's the recipient of a New York Foundation for the Arts Fellowship in playwriting. Her poetry was part of the Aldrich Museum's 1996 exhibition No Doubt: African American Art of the 90s.

Benson's work has also appeared in magazines and books. Her teleplay *Hair Story* was aired on Lifetime in May 2001, and her plays have included the one-woman show, *Boxed,* as well as several pieces that deal with a mythical town in Texas.

SUGGESTED READING

Benson's work appears in the following anthologies:
In the Tradition: An Anthology of Young Black Writers (edited by Ras Baraka and Kevin Powell; Writers and Readers)
Verses That Hurt: Pleasure and Pain from the Poemfone Poets (edited by Jordan Trachtenberg; St. Martin's Press)
Lest We Forget (Drum FM; CD recording)

CLAIRE BRAZ-VALENTINE (b. 1939) is a widely published playwright and poet, and has worked in the California Prison Arts Program for the past 10 years. The "Flipped on Its Axis" excerpts featured in *The Body Eclectic* are true stories taken from her poetic play, *Listen to Our Voices.* This play was written through storytelling improvisations at the Redwoods Treatment Center in Santa Cruz County, California. Redwoods is a lockdown facility for addicted teens who have broken the law and been made wards of the court.

SUGGESTED READING

This One Thing I Do (play; Samuel French, Inc.)

KIM LY BUI-BURTON (b. 1958) spent the first two years of her life in Vietnam. The daughter of a Vietnamese educator and a German-American nurse, she grew up without poems or stories that reflected her family's rich history. A poet and public librarian, Bui-Burton celebrates and promotes many diverse voices in her work. Her poems have appeared in several anthologies. She lives with her family in the Central Coast area of California.

Bui-Burton's poems appear in the following anthology: *Tilting the Continent: Southeast Asian American Writing* (edited by Shirley Lim and Cheng Lok Chua; New Rivers Press)

GEORGE GORDON, LORD BYRON (1788–1824) inherited his grand title at the age of 10. Its benefit of revenues allowed him to live a dissolute life of luxury and to indulge his every pleasure. His debauchery scandalized his native England and identified him in the public mind as the prototype of the Romantic hero he wrote about.

Although subject to deep depressions and drawn to taboo behaviors, Byron was also affable, loyal to his friends and servants, engaged with the life of his times, and deeply committed to liberal political causes. He pursued the latter at his own peril in Parliament, Italian politics, and finally in the 1821 Greek revolt against the Turks, supplying and leading his own regiment to the Greek mainland, where he died of a mysterious fever in 1824.

Despite being identified as a Romantic poet, Byron despised the movement and wrote scathingly about Wordsworth, Coleridge, and Sir Walter Scott, among others. His own work was almost completely written in the "old-fashioned" modes of the eighteenth century, particularly his penchant for satires in the vein of Pope, Swift, and Voltaire. Even his celebrated love poem included in this anthology, "She Walks in Beauty," is in reality an elaborate love compliment in the manner of the eighteenth-century Cavalier poets. Byron was easily the most read and internationally admired English poet of his time—one of his books sold 10,000 copies on the day it was published—but his literary reputation suffered greatly in the twentieth century.

SUGGESTED READING

The Love Poems of Lord Byron: A Romantic's Passion (St. Martin's Press)

Lord Byron: The Major Works (edited by Jerome J. McGann; Oxford University Press)

LEWIS CARROLL (1832–1898) is the pseudonym of the Reverend Charles Lutwidge Dodgson, a mathematics lecturer at Oxford University, but he is better known to the world as the author of *Alice's Adventures in Wonderland*, which was first published in 1865.

Carroll was a complex figure, and much of our understanding of him has been based on a limited knowledge of his life. Many of his personal papers were destroyed by his family after his death, and his letters and journals did not become available until the second half of the twentieth century. For years he'd been considered "simple-hearted," and a man who had an inappropriate interest in girls and young women. A myth was formed based on that assumption. But the latest scholarship, particularly that of the book *In the Shadow of the Dreamchild: A New Understanding of Lewis Carroll*, by Karoline Leach, presents him as "a mature, complex, contradictory, and mysterious personality, whose 'unconventional' relationships with women caused gossip and scandal in his own time." In a letter, Carroll wrote, "You need not be shocked at my being spoken against. Anybody, who is spoken of at all, is sure to be spoken against by somebody." Whoever he was in his personal life, he wrote what is now a classic of children's literature, and for many readers, it is a favorite childhood book.

SUGGESTED READING

Alice's Adventures in Wonderland/Through the Looking Glass and What Alice Found There (John Tenniel, illustrator; William Morrow & Co.)

Humorous Verse of Lewis Carroll (Dover Publications)
In the Shadow of the Dreamchild: A New Understanding of Lewis Carroll (biography by Karoline Leach; Dufour Editions)
Lewis Carroll: Poetry for Young People (Sterling Publications)

ELIZABETH CARTER (1717–1806) was a poet and translator from England. Under the pen name Eliza, she contributed for years to the *Gentleman's Magazine*. Collections of her poems were published in 1738 and 1762, and her translations of Epictetus were published in 1758. Carter knew 10 languages and was said to have dreamed in Arabic and Hebrew. She was one of the group of women known as the Bluestockings. During the first half of the eighteenth century, English women usually received little education and had no intellectual status. It was considered unbecoming for them to know Greek or Latin, and inappropriate for them to be authors. Originally, the Bluestockings were British women intellectuals of high social standing—several were society hostesses. The term *bluestocking* came to be used derogatorily for a woman who placed learning and displaying knowledge above her femininity.

SANDRA CISNEROS (b. 1954), poet, novelist, short-story writer, and essayist, is a Chicana writer whose work has received great acclaim. Her book of short stories, *The House on Mango Street*, won the American Book Award from the Before Columbus Foundation. Born in Chicago, the only daughter among seven children, Cisneros earned her B.A. from Loyola University and her M.A. from the Writers' Workshop at the University of Iowa in 1978. In her fiction she writes about her heritage, giving voice to Chicano life and culture. She has also written about her experiences of alienation, loneliness, and degradation. Cisneros has contributed to many magazines, including *Glamour*,

The New York Times, and *Revista Chicano-Riquena.* She's received fellowships from the National Endowment for the Arts and the MacArthur Foundation. Cisneros has taught at many colleges and universities, including the University of California, University of Michigan, and the University of New Mexico. She lives in San Antonio, Texas.

About incorporating Spanish explicitly into her work, Cisneros says, "I think that . . . allows me to create new expressions in English—to say things in English that have never been said before. . . . You can say a phrase in Spanish, and you can choose to not translate it, but you can make it understood through the context." Her favorite writers include Merce Rodoreda, Grace Paley, and Manuel Puig.

SUGGESTED READING

The House on Mango Street (short stories; Vintage Books)
Loose Woman: Poems (Vintage Books)
Woman Hollering Creek and Other Stories (Vintage Books)

LUCILLE CLIFTON (b. 1936) was born in New York to a mother who was a launderer, homemaker, and avocational poet, and to a father who worked in the steel mills. Clifton's parents had a great appreciation for books, which they passed on to her. She began college when she was 16 and went to Howard University, as the first person in her family to finish high school and enter college. Langston Hughes was the first to publish Clifton's work, in the anthology *Poetry of the Negro.* She has received the National Book Award and the Juniper Prize, and twice has been nominated for the Pulitzer Prize for her poetry. Clifton is also the author of more than 20 children's books. She currently lives in Maryland.

Clifton tells a story of performing in an annual Christmas program when she was five years old and forgetting her piece. She says, "I remember standing there on stage in my new Christmas dress, trying not to cry as the church members smiled, nodded, and murmured encouragement from the front row. . . . But I couldn't remember, and to hide my deep humiliation, my embarrassment, I became sullen, angry. . . . It was a scandal! . . . Then, like a great tidal wave from the ocean of God, my sanctified mother poured down the Baptist aisle, huge as love, her hand outstretched toward mine. . . . She smiled, then turned to address the church: 'She don't have to do nothing she don't want to do.'"

SUGGESTED READING

Good Woman: Poems and a Memoir 1969–1980 (BOA Editions, Ltd.)

The Book of Light (poems; BOA Editions, Ltd.)

Blessing the Boats: New and Selected Poems (BOA Editions, Ltd.)

STEPHEN DOBYNS (b. 1941) is from New Jersey. He graduated from Wayne State University and earned an M.F.A. from the University of Iowa. He is the author of 10 books of poetry and 20 novels. He has received the Lamont Poetry Selection of the Academy of American Poets, and fellowships from the National Endowment for the Arts and the Guggenheim Foundation. His novels have been translated into more than 10 languages. Dobyns has taught at a number of colleges and universities, including the University of Iowa and Boston University. He lives in Boston with his wife and three children.

In an interview Dobyns said, "Language is always communication. If I'm writing something, I'm also writing something that I want to be read. It doesn't need to be read today, but it holds out the promise to me that it will be read. Whatever it is, the story, poem, whatever, is also then a kind of argument."

SUGGESTED READING

Best Words, Best Order: Essays on Poetry (St. Martin's Press)
Boy in the Water (novel; Holt/Metropolitan)
Common Carnage (poems; Viking Penguin)
Velocities: New and Selected Poems, 1966–1992 (Penguin)

MARK DOTY (b. 1953) is the author of five books of poems. He has received the Ambassador Book Award, the Bingham Poetry Prize, a Lambda Literary Award, and the National Book Critics Circle Award. He has received fellowships from the Guggenheim, Ingram Merrill, Rockefeller, and Whiting foundations, as well as from the National Endowment for the Arts. Doty alternately lives in Provincetown, Massachusetts, and Houston, Texas, where he teaches at the University of Houston.

About poetry Doty says, "I, for one, am hungry to read poems of American life now, in all its messy complications, with its terrors and uncertainties and possible grounds for hope. . . . The work of the poet investigating personal experience is always to find such points of connection, to figure out how to open the private out to the reader."

SUGGESTED READING

Heaven's Coast: A Memoir (HarperCollins)
Still Life with Oysters and Lemon (essays; Beacon Press)
Sweet Machine (poems; HarperCollins)

PAUL LAURENCE DUNBAR (1872–1906) was one of the first African-American poets to gain national recognition. His parents, Joshua and Matilda Murphy Dunbar, were freed slaves from Kentucky, and Dunbar drew on their stories of plantation life throughout his writing career. His first poems were published when he was 14. Although he was a good student, he was financially unable to go to college, and instead got a job as an elevator operator. In 1893 Dunbar self-published a collection of poems called *Oak and Ivy*. To help pay the costs of publishing his book, he sold copies for a dollar to people riding in his elevator. He was friends with Frederick Douglass, who said that Dunbar was "the most promising young colored man in America." By 1895 Dunbar's poems began appearing in major national magazines and newspapers, such as the *New York Times*. His second collection of poems, *Majors and Minors*, was published with the help of friends. The poems he'd written in standard English he called "majors," and those in dialect he called "minors." It was the dialect poems, however, that brought Dunbar the most attention. He toured England reading his poetry. When he came back to the United States, Dunbar received a clerkship at the Library of Congress in Washington, D.C., and shortly thereafter, he married the writer Alice Ruth Moore. He continued writing poetry, as well as short stories and a novel. He also wrote lyrics to a number of musical reviews. In 1898 Dunbar's health deteriorated, and he left his job to dedicate himself full-time to writing and to giving readings. He died at the age of 33.

SUGGESTED READING

The Collected Poems of Paul Laurence Dunbar (University of Virginia Press)

Paul Laurence Dunbar: Portrait of a Poet (biography, young adults; Enslow Publishers)

CORNELIUS EADY (b. 1954) is the author of six books of poems. *Victims of the Latest Dance Craze* won the Lamont Prize from the Academy of American Poets, and his book *The Gathering of My Name* was nominated for the Pulitzer Prize. He is the recipient of a National Endowment for the Arts Fellowship in literature, a Guggenheim Fellowship in poetry, and a Rockefeller Foundation Fellowship to Bellagio, Italy. His work appears in many journals and anthologies. He has taught poetry extensively, including at SUNY at Stony Brook, Sarah Lawrence College, New York University, and the 92nd Street Y. A theater production of his most recent book of poems, *Brutal Imagination*, was performed at The Kitchen in New York City.

SUGGESTED READING

Autobiography of a Jukebox (poems; Carnegie-Mellon University Press)

Brutal Imagination (poems; Putnam Publishing Group)

ANITA ENDREZZE (b. 1952) is a poet, writer, and artist of mixed heritage. She is half Yaqui Indian and half European. In her most recent book, *Throwing Fire at the Sun, Water at the Moon*, Endrezze traces her family and tribal history through stories, myths, journal extracts, and art. She is presently at work on a book set in Mexico in the 1500s.

Endrezze says, "For many years I was skinny, and the only attention I paid to 'the body' was in the context of how a poem looked (its shape, and the function of that shape, which was usually long and skinny). Now, in middle age I've gained a few extra pounds, and I find myself writing novels!"

SUGGESTED READING

Throwing Fire at the Sun, Water at the Moon (University of Arizona Press)

TESS GALLAGHER (b. 1943) was born in Port Angeles, Washington, where she lives today in a home she calls Sky House, which she designed and built for herself. She is the daughter of a logger and longshoreman. She graduated from the University of Washington and received her M.F.A. from the

University of Iowa in 1974. Gallagher is the author of several books of poems and two collections of short stories. She has taught at many colleges, including Bucknell University and Whitman College. Gallagher was married to the fiction writer and poet Raymond Carver, who died an early death in 1988.

About poems Gallagher says, "They seem . . . like provisional rafts I've thrown together out of the debris of my situations. When I've been most devastated in my life, I've fallen entirely silent, as I did the first six months after Ray's death." Much of her poetry focuses on the passage of time and the nature of memory. Her advice to writers includes, "[D]on't limit your choice of artistic medium—prose, poetry, photography, film, painting—too early in your life."

SUGGESTED READING

Amplitude: New and Selected Poems (Graywolf Press)
A Concert of Tenses: Essays on Poetry (Poets on Poetry Series, University of Michigan Press)
Moon Crossing Bridge (poems; Graywolf Press)

ALICIA GASPAR DE ALBA (b. 1958) received her Ph.D. from the University of New Mexico in 1994. Her book *Sor Juana's Second Dream* won the Best Historical Fiction Award from the Latino Literary Hall of Fame in 2000, and she is also a recipient of the Border-Ford/Pellicer-Frost Award for poetry. Gaspar de Alba is currently an associate professor of Chicana/o Studies at UCLA. She shares her life with Deena Gonzalez.

Gaspar de Alba writes this about her poem: "'Making Tortillas' is about lesbian lovemaking. In Latin America, a colloquial term for *lesbian* is 'tortillera,' or 'tortilla maker,' which has something to do with the sound of hands clapping wet cornmeal into the shape of a tortilla. Although I am a Chicana from the border in El Paso, Texas, I had never heard this expression until I went to Iowa City to begin course work for my Ph.D. There, I was welcomed into a community of Cuban, Puerto Rican, Argentinian, and other Latino-identified gay men and lesbians, and it was among this group that I heard the term for the first time and knew I would have to write a poem about making tortillas as lesbian love."

SUGGESTED READING

Sor Juana's Second Dream (novel; University of New Mexico Press)

The Mystery of Survival and Other Stories (Bilingual Press)

"Beggar on the Cordoba Bridge" (a collection of poems in *Three Times a Woman: Chicana Poetry*; Bilingual Press)

REGINALD GIBBONS (b. 1947) was born and grew up in Houston, Texas. He studied piano and also played clarinet, performing as a piano accompanist and occasionally as a soloist in contests and school concerts. He received a B.A. in Spanish from Princeton University, an M.A. in English and creative writing from Stanford University, and a Ph.D. in comparative literature from Stanford. He is the author of six books of poetry, and he teaches English at Northwestern University and creative writing in the M.F.A. Program for Writers at Warren Wilson College.

Gibbons writes, "'Breath' was based on a sudden unexpected memory of something I used to do when I was at a neighborhood swimming pool, when I was perhaps 12 years old—which was to let all the breath out of my skinny body and swim down to the bottom in the deep end and lie there, looking up at the other swimmers for a few seconds, and listening to the water-muffled sounds of their voices and their swimming and diving. What made this memory the seed of a poem was that I also suddenly saw how that strange, self-risking moment of escape must have been provoked by something deep and painful in my life as a child, and then I remembered what that was, or might have been. The poem comes out of a memory of something lived, but is not written in order to try to tell that memory accurately; instead, the poem tries to find where feelings are connected to each other, in the poet."

SUGGESTED READING
Homage to Longshot O'Leary (poems; Holy Cow Press)
Selected Poems of Luis Cernuda (translated by Reginald Gibbons; Sheep Meadow Press)
Sparrow: New and Selected Poems (Louisiana State University Press)

MELINDA GOODMAN (b. 1957) is a poet, novelist, and teacher. She has taught poetry workshops at Hunter College in New York City for the past 15 years.

Goodman writes, "'Cobwebs' is about the common experience of how a child loves to go through her mother's things. You can tell a lot about somebody by looking at their possessions. For instance, the 'gold cigarette lighter/with the built-in watch' is ironic because my mom had a self-destructive habit of smoking. The watch part of the lighter is a symbol of time ticking away on her life as she lights up.

"The poem is also about having a mother who could be very seductive and very 'flip' in her style of parenting. She didn't think anything of washing her children and her lingerie at the same time. She sometimes treated the kids more like objects or chores than as children with needs and personalities. My mother never taught me to be gentle with my body and to cherish it."

LUCY GREALY (b. 1963) was born in Dublin, Ireland. She survived a 20-year period of overwhelming physical and mental suffering due to a rare facial-bone cancer that she was diagnosed with at the age of nine. She lost a third of her jaw to this cancer and underwent two and a half years of chemotherapy and radiation treatments. Her book *Autobiography of a Face* chronicles this experience. Teased horribly in school, Grealy says, "I . . . was naturally adept at protecting myself from the hurt of their insults and felt a vague superiority. . . ."

SUGGESTED READING

As Seen on TV: Provocations (essays; Bloomsbury Publishers)
Autobiography of a Face (memoir; HarperPerennial Library)

DONALD HALL (b. 1928) is the author of 14 books of poetry, most recently *The Painted Bed*. He has also written children's books, plays, essays, and a memoir. In 1992 he received the Robert Frost Silver Medal from the Poetry Society of America, and in 1994, the Lily Prize for Poetry. Three of Hall's books have been nominated for the National Book Award. He served as Poet Laureate of New Hampshire for several years.

Hall writes, "'Eating the Pig' came with a rush, and only took about six months to finish. I remember being so excited, at the onset of this poem, that I actually dictated notes for it. Notes, I think, not lines. It was the morning after the party at which we ate the suckling pig. It was also around the time of the final American evacuation of Vietnam. All my long life, I suppose beginning with newsreels at movie houses during the Spanish Civil War, I have seen in photographs the weary lines of refugees fleeing the enemy. It is an emblem of the last century.

"Poetry is written and read by the body, and received through the mouth. It is read by the mouth, not by the eyes or ears, and it goes directly to the stomach."

SUGGESTED READING

The Old Life (poems; Houghton Mifflin)

To Read a Poem (nonfiction; Harcourt Brace College and School Division)

Writing Well (nonfiction; Addison-Wesley)

THOMAS HARDY (1840–1928) was born near Dorchester in southwest England, the "Wessex" of his novels. He worked as an architect in London but was unable to suppress his love of literature and writing, and at the age of 31, published his first novel. Fifteen other novels followed, intriguing prose dramas steeped in characters at the mercy of both their passions and an indifferent universe, where chance and irony rule and even the humblest peasant's life takes on tragic dimensions. Most of the novels were immensely popular, allowing Hardy to write full-time. But when his last novel, *Jude the Obscure* (1896), was brutally criticized in the press, Hardy turned in disgust from fiction to poetry, publishing his first volume of balladlike lyrics in 1898 when he was 58. Seven volumes of poetry followed, and today he is considered one of the leading English poets of the twentieth century. His attention to the landscapes, characters, and physical details of nineteenth-century British rural life of all classes continues to fascinate readers to this day.

SUGGESTED READING

Selected Poems (Everyman Paperback Classics)

Tess of the D'Urbervilles (novel; Bantam)

The Woodlanders (novel; Everyman's Library)

WILLIAM J. HARRIS (b. 1942) teaches American and African-American literature and creative writing at Penn State University. He writes, "'Rib Sandwich' talks about how you can physically walk out of America without ever leaving America. My favorite poet is Amiri Baraka; my favorite composers are Mozart and John Coltrane."

SUGGESTED READING

The Leroi Jones/Amiri Baraka Reader (edited by William J. Harris; Thunder's Mouth Press/Nation Books)

Call & Response: The Riverside Anthology of the African American Literary Tradition (coedited by William J. Harris; Houghton Mifflin)

KEELYN T. HEALY (b. 1975) began writing poetry in high school in Gig Harbor, Washington. Reading the poets Lucille Clifton and Sharon Olds inspired her to take risks in her own writing. Healy writes, "Suddenly I had given myself permission to write about all the previously 'taboo' issues I had always wanted to comment on." It was when a girl on her college soccer team died that Healy began to take her writing seriously.

Healy studied in Italy for three years, and she will soon graduate with a master's degree from the University of Southern California. Her poems have appeared in the *Seattle Review, Southern California Review, Spillway, Faultline Journal*, and *Allegheny Review*.

MIGUEL HERNÁNDEZ (1910–1942) was born into a peasant family in Spain. He had little education but published his first book when he was only 23. In 1934 he published his first play. He became friends with writers such as Federico García Lorca, Pablo Neruda, Luis Cernuda, and many others. Hernández worked with Neruda on the publication of the influential journal *Caballo Verde para la Poesía/Green Horse of Poetry*, and became involved with a group of writers supporting the Republican cause. In 1937 he married his boyhood sweetheart, Josefina Manresa. During the Spanish Civil War, Hernández served in the Republican army. He wrote about the horror of the war in his poetry. In 1939, while trying to flee to Portugal, he was arrested and imprisoned for opposing Franco. Even in prison he continued to write, and the poems of this period are considered by many to be his most important. One of these, "Lullaby of the Onion" ("Nanas de la Cebolla"), was for his son, which he wrote after having received a letter from his wife saying that she had only bread and onions to eat. His hope, expressed in the poem, is that his baby son will grow strong from her milk made of onions. He died in prison on March 28, 1942.

SUGGESTED READING

I Have Lots of Heart (poems; Dufour Editions)
The Unending Light: Selected Poems (Sheep Meadow Press)

BARBARA HILL (b. 1951) is a journalist, freelance writer, and poet. She was born in Trieste, Italy, to an Italian mother and an Arkansas farm boy father. She wrote her first short story when she was 10 years old, and has been writing ever since. Hill makes her home in San Jose, California.

She says, "Writing is my body stretching and bending toward light and shadow. I become antsy and irritable when I don't write, find myself stumbling into furniture, tripping over my own feet. Once I sit down and put pen to paper, I feel each word, like a solitary rock, slowly roll onto the page. That is when my body relaxes and settles into itself."

JANE HIRSHFIELD (b. 1953) is the author of several books of poems, as well as a book of essays and two collections of poetry in translation. She is the recipient of the Poetry Center Book Award, the Bay Area Book Award, and fellowships from the Guggenheim and Rockefeller Foundations. She lives in the San Francisco Bay Area.

Hirshfield says, "I see poetry as a path toward new understanding and transformation, so I've looked at specific poems I love, and at poetry's gestures in the broadest sense, in an effort to feel and learn what they offer from the inside."

SUGGESTED READING
Given Sugar, Given Salt (poems; HarperCollins)
Nine Gates: Entering the Mind of Poetry (essays; Harper-
   Perennial Library)

LINDA HOGAN (b. 1947), Chickasaw poet, short-story writer, novelist, playwright, essayist, and environmentalist, grew up in Oklahoma and lives in Colorado. She was raised in a military family and therefore moved often. Hogan is a professor of English at the University of Colorado in Boulder, where she received her M.A. in 1978. She has served on the National Endowment for the Arts poetry panel for two years and has been involved in wildlife rehabilitation as a volunteer. Hogan has played a prominent role in the development of contemporary Native-American poetry, particularly in its relationship to environmental and antinuclear issues. The honors for her work include the Five Civilized Tribes Playwriting Award, Guggenheim Award, the Lannan Award, and a fellowship from the National Endowment for the Arts.

SUGGESTED READING
The Book of Medicines (poems; Coffee House Press)
Power: A Novel (W. W. Norton)
Solar Storms: A Novel (Scribner)
Woman Who Watches Over the World: A Native Memoir
   (W. W. Norton)

MARIE HOWE (b. 1950) works primarily as a poet and teacher of poetry. She's on the faculty of the Columbia University School of the Arts in New York City. Howe is a recipient of the Peter Lavin Younger Poets Prize and fellowships from the National Endowment for the Arts and the Bunting Institute at Radcliffe College. She teaches in the graduate department at Sarah Lawrence College and is a visiting faculty member at New York University.

SUGGESTED READING
The Good Thief (poems; Persea Books)
In the Company of My Solitude: American Writing from the AIDS Pandemic (anthology; coedited by Marie Howe with M. Klein; Persea Books)
What the Living Do: Poems (W. W. Norton)

ERIN JOHNSON (b. 1986) is 15 and a high-school sophomore, home-schooling in Santa Cruz, California, after having attended Waldorf School for her prior education.

Johnson says, "I do not feel a great connection between poetry and the physical body. Rather, I have always felt that poetry transports me to another place while still remaining deeply rooted in self. Poetry has been a sustaining force in my life because with it, I can take pain, anger, or ugliness and illuminate them with, if not beauty, a semblance of form. Poetry is the divine outlet that has preserved my sanity."

MAURICE KENNY (b. 1929), recipient of the American Book Award, is the author of several books. His new collection of poems is *In the Time of the Present.* Mr. Kenny teaches at SUNY, Potsdam, and lives in Saranac Lake in the Adirondack Mountains.

About "Legacy," Kenny writes, "Without explicating my

poem and taking away its true spirit, allow me to say the following: I have always been close to Mother Earth. As a boy I spent many summers on the farm in the berry fields, in hay fields, the garden, and the woods, which were always abundant with not only trees but particular trees—conifers, and nut trees such as hickory and butternut—and of course various animals. I spent much of my childhood also on the shores of Lake Ontario at Chaumont Bay in northern New York State. A lone though not lonely child, I roamed fields and streams, and as I grew older, I grew closer to Mother Earth, nature. I began to recognize that I as a human being was a strong and important part—I am grass, I am bird, I am fish, I am tree—and that all these great gifts of the Creator are also a part of me. Consequently I wanted these wonders to endure in complete form. This would be my legacy, not only as a human being but as a creative poet, a singer of songs. This is the essential of the poem."

SUGGESTED READING

Backward to Forward: Prose Pieces (White Pine Press)

Tekonwatonti: Molly Brant: 1735–1795 (poems; White Pine Press)

On Second Thought: A Compilation (anthology; edited by Maurice Kenny with Joseph Bruchac; University of Oklahoma Press)

In the Time of the Present: New Poems (Michigan State University Press)

GALWAY KINNELL (b. 1927) was born in Rhode Island and studied at Princeton and the University of Rochester. He served in the U.S. Navy, and after that, went to Paris on a Fulbright Fellowship. The author of many books of poems, Kinnell won the Pulitzer Prize for poetry in 1983. He alternately lives in Vermont and New York City, and is a professor of creative writing at New York University. He is currently a chancellor of the Academy of American Poets.

Kinnell's introduction to poetry occurred when he was a boy: "I came to love poetry when I discovered, in a little anthology in my parents' bookshelf, the poems of Edgar Allan Poe in particular. . . . To discover that this language could sing like that—'It was many and many a year ago, / In a kingdom by the sea, . . .'—thrilled me. I had a particularly lonely childhood, not in the sense of not having people around, but failing to make real connections and being shy to the point of mutinous, so the solitaries among the poets, like Dickinson and Poe, appealed to me a lot. . . . One thing that leads a person to poetry is an inner life of some activity and maybe even turbulence, the weight of meaning and feeling that has to get out."

SUGGESTED READING

The Essential Rilke (translated by Galway Kinnell with
    H. Liebmann; Ecco Press)
Mortal Acts, Mortal Words (poems; Houghton Mifflin)
A New Selected Poems (Houghton Mifflin)

STEVE KOWIT's (b. 1938) poem, "In the Morning," comes from *Passionate Journey,* a collection of his adaptations of Indian love poetry. Kowit says, "I have tried to capture the lingering magic of a kiss, of an evening remembered dreamily in the morning. There are a thousand ways to let another person know you admire him or her—and each one is a gift that enriches that other person's life, and no doubt your own."

SUGGESTED READING

In the Palm of Your Hand: The Poet's Portable Workshop
    (Tilbury House)
Passionate Journey (poems; City Miner Books)

LI-YOUNG LEE (b. 1957) was born in Jakarta, Indonesia, of Chinese parents. His father, who was a personal physician to Mao Tse-tung while in China, had relocated his family to Indonesia. In 1959 his family fled the country to escape anti-Chinese sentiment and, after a five-year trek through Hong Kong, Macau, and Japan, they settled in the United States in 1964. Li-Young Lee attended Pittsburgh and Arizona Universities, and the State University of New York. He has taught at several schools, including Northwestern and the University of Iowa.

His book *The City in Which I Love You* was the 1990 Lamont Poetry Selection and won the Delmore Schwartz Memorial Poetry Award. His memoir, *The Winged Seed: A Remembrance*, received an American Book Award from the Before Columbus Foundation. His other honors include a Lannan Literary Award, a Whiting Writer's Award, a grant from the National Endowment for the Arts, and a Guggenheim Foundation Fellowship. He lives in Chicago with his wife, Donna, and their two sons.

SUGGESTED READING

Book of My Nights (poems; BOA Editions, Ltd.)
The City in Which I Love You (poems; BOA Editions, Ltd.)
Rose (BOA Editions, Ltd.)
The Winged Seed: A Remembrance (Simon & Schuster)

LYN LIFSHIN's (b. 1944) most recent book, *Before It's Light*, won the Paterson Poetry Award. She has published more than 100 books of poetry, and her poems have appeared in literary magazines. She is the subject of an award-winning documentary film, *Lyn Lifshin: Not Made of Glass*, available from Women Make Movies.

Lifshin writes this about "Fat": "I probably never was as fat as I thought I was, even at six years old when I longed to be as skinny and straight-haired as my snobby, spoiled cousin Elaine. Growing up in a small Vermont town where my family was one of only a few Jewish families, we always felt like outsiders, different. Once when I saw 'kike' on the blackboard I was sure it was not only because I was Jewish but also because I was fat. Eventually I became quite thin. I never really dieted: divorce, sickness, other stress has whittled me into the 100-pound woman most comfortable in miniskirts (to run to the metro). But at times I still, in spite of enough attention, somewhere deep down, keep waiting to be asked to dance. Unlike most poems I write, much in 'Fat' is true. My underpants did snap on Main Street, and I did bicycle madly hoping to lose weight."

SUGGESTED READING

Before It's Light (poems; Black Sparrow Press)

Cold Comfort: Selected Poems 1970–1996 (Black Sparrow Press)

Tangled Vines: A Collection of Mother and Daughter Poems (edited by Lyn Lifshin; Harvest Books)

MORTON MARCUS (b. 1936) was born and raised in New York City but has lived in California since 1961. His poetry has appeared in many literary journals and in more than 75 anthologies. He is the author of nine books of poetry and one novel. His most recent books, both published in 2002, are *Moments Without Names: New & Selected Prose Poems* and *Shouting Down the Silence.*

Although all of Marcus's poetry is highly accessible and contains unexpected imagery, each of his books is different in style and approach, from the short nature lyrics of *The Santa Cruz Mountain Poems* to the narrative history of his family in *Pages from a Scapbook of Immigrants* to the whimsical prose poems of *When People Could Fly*.

Marcus says, "We learn everything through our bodies, through our senses: eyes, nose, ears, fingers, tongue. And yet we take the sense organs and the body in general for granted. I've written many poems about body parts over the years in order to awaken awareness in myself and in the reader to the wonder of the body and how it works, and how it is the necessary springboard we must catapult from in order to enter the lives of others and to soar into the world of the spirit."

SUGGESTED READING

Moments Without Names: New & Selected Prose Poems
  (White Pine Press)
Shouting Down the Silence (poems; Creative Arts)

LIN MAX (b. 1946) has a B.A. in Literature from the University of California, Davis, and graduate degrees in English Literature and Librarianship. She lives in Northern California, where she studies piano and paints. Her poems have appeared in anthologies and in many journals, including *Calyx: A Journal for Art and Literature by Women, Iris,* and *Iowa Woman*.

About "This Part of Your Body," Max writes, "I wrote the poem when my niece, Annie, was 12 years old and had just had her first period. My sister had told me on the phone that Annie wouldn't touch 'that part of her body.' That comment popped into my mind a few days later when I was writing in my early-morning journal, and I wrote the poem very quickly and spontaneously. These early A.M. poems, drafted between five and six, before I get out of bed, have a special kind of energy, honesty, and rhythm. Annie is now 23 and in the Peace Corps in West Africa. I'm going to write her today and remind her to love her body fiercely, every part of it, because she's going to be living in it, as we all do, for a long time."

Max's poems appear in the following anthologies:
Claiming the Spirit Within: A Sourcebook of Women's Poetry
(edited by Marilyn Sewell; Beacon Press)
Mixed Voices: Contemporary Poems About Music (edited by
E. Buchwald and R. Roston; Milkweed Editions)

JANICE MIRIKITANI (b. 1941) was born the year that Americans of Japanese ancestry were incarcerated in American concentration camps. She and her family were interned in the Rohwer, Arkansas, relocation camp during World War II. She graduated with honors from UCLA and received her teaching credentials from the University of California at Berkeley. A sansei (third-generation) Japanese American, she is a poet, editor, and community activist. She is the executive director of Glide Memorial Church. Mirikitani has been named San Francisco's Poet Laureate for 2001. She is the editor of *I Have Something to Say About This: Children of the Tenderloin Speak Out*, the first collection of children's writings to come out of the crack-cocaine crisis. *Watch Out, We're Talking: Speaking Out About Incest and Abuse* is a compilation of oral histories and written testimonies by women and men who experienced childhood incest and abuse.

Mirikitani writes, "Doreen was inspired by a living person, who seemed to fully loathe herself, loud and boisterous, but tender and needing affection. Doreen is the mirror of my own self-hatred. I, in my moments of self-rejection, feel I understand Doreen's contempt for her flesh, which is like a scar of our *difference* from white people. In my past, I internalized all the racist jokes and slurs about our eyes and flat faces and bodies—about how our plumbing ran horizontally, and I felt ashamed. My emotional pursuit was to gain the acceptance of white society. I thought if I only looked more like them or married a white man, I would gain vicarious power."

SUGGESTED READING

I Have Something to Say About This: Children of the Tenderloin Speak Out (anthology; Glide Word Press)

Watch Out, We're Talking: Speaking Out About Incest and Abuse (anthology; Glide Word Press)

PABLO NERUDA (1904–1973) was born to a poor family in rural Chile. His *Twenty Love Poems and a Song of Despair,* published in 1924, established him as a poet of importance and earned him a place in the Chilean diplomatic corps, a profession that took him to the Far East in the late twenties and early thirties and to Spain in 1935, a year before the outbreak of the Spanish Civil War. In Spain he befriended the great Spanish poets of the time, including Federico García Lorca. When he publicly defended the Spanish Republican cause against the Fascist insurgents, to the embarrassment of the Chilean government, he was forced to resign his post.

In his poetry Neruda speaks to and for the common person, and his work expresses the struggle of workers and his deep love for his country. In 1945 Neruda was elected to the Chilean senate, but had to flee the country when the government was taken over by right-wing extremists. He returned when a new government came to power and moved to a house on Isla Negra with the great love of his life, Matilde Urrutia. By this time, he was a national hero and an international celebrity. He spent the last 20 years of his life continuing to mine the rich vein of his literary imagination and received many international awards, among them, the Stalin Prize and the Nobel Prize. He died of leukemia in 1973, although it is said he also died of a broken heart, following the murder that same year of his friend, Salvador Allende, Chile's president, during a right-wing coup.

Captain's Verses (translated by Donald D. Walsh; New Directions Press)

Memoirs (translated by Hardie St. Martin; Farrar, Straus & Giroux)

Selected Odes of Pablo Neruda (translated by Margaret Sayers Peden; University of California Press)

Twenty Love Poems and a Song of Despair (translated by W. S. Merwin; Chronicle Books)

ANDREW NIELSEN (b. 1982) is a student at Stanford University. He sees himself more as a performer than a writer. "I no longer have acne and am very happy about that," he reports. "I wrote this poem because pimples are such an irritating thing that they can ruin your whole day and make you feel worthless. A good way to deal with things that bother you is to write about them, so writing this poem was cathartic."

SHARON OLDS (b. 1942) was born in San Francisco and raised, as she says, a "hellfire Calvinist." She received her B.A. from Stanford and her Ph.D. from Columbia University. After graduating, she vowed to become a poet, to find her own voice. And she asked, "Is there anything that shouldn't or can't be written about in a poem? What has never been written in a poem?" She set out to write some of those poems herself, and in her work she breaks silence and tells intimate truths about family and the body, and how people in her family treated one another in ways that are often startling and sometimes so revealing and frank they may be discomforting. The poet Michael Ondaatje says that Olds's poems are "pure fire in the hands." She teaches poetry workshops in the Graduate Creative Writing Program at New

York University and helps run the NYU workshop program at Godwater Hospital in New York. She was the New York State Poet Laureate from 1998 to 2000.

SUGGESTED READING
Blood, Tin, Straw (poems; Knopf)
The Dead and the Living (poems; Random House)
The Gold Cell (poems; Knopf)

The OSAGE poem "Planting Initiation Song" is a woman's song dating to the turn of the nineteenth century. The Osage are a Native-American tribe who were originally from the Midwest. The women were responsible for planting, cultivating, and harvesting. The "Plantation Initiation Song" was translated and recorded by the anthropologist Francis La Flesche.

SUGGESTED READING
The Osage: Indians of North America (young-adult nonfiction; by Terry P. Wilson; Chelsea House Publishing)

MARGE PIERCY (b. 1936) is a poet and novelist, an essayist, and a feminist. Piercy was active in both the civil rights and the anti-Vietnam war movements during the 1960s. In her early twenties she held a variety of jobs to make ends meet, including department-store clerk and switchboard operator. After moving to Cape Cod in 1971, she was able to create a life balanced between writing, gardening, and political activism. In 1997 she and her husband established a small literary publishing house, Leapfrog Press. Her literary influences include William Carlos Williams, Pablo Neruda, Edith Sitwell, and Allen Ginsberg.

Piercy says, "The difference between novels and poetry? It is the difference between diamonds and elephants. . . . Poetry, to me, is the creation of this artifact made of human utterance. It arises somehow more directly out of human experience, and it aims to clarify, preserve, and communicate that experience."

SUGGESTED READING

Mars and Her Children (poems; Knopf)

So You Want to Write (nonfiction; with Ira Woods; Leapfrog Press)

What Are Big Girls Made Of? (poems; Knopf)

MINNIE BRUCE PRATT'S (b. 1946) second book of poetry, *Crime Against Nature*, was chosen as the 1989 Lamont Poetry Selection by the Academy of American Poets, and received the American Library Association's Gay and Lesbian Book Award for literature. She coauthored the essay "Identity: Skin Blood Heart," a feminist classic that appeared in *Yours in Struggle: Three Feminist Perspectives on Anti-Semitism and Racism*, a book she coedited. Her book *S/HE* is a collection of stories about gender-boundary crossing.

Pratt says, "I wrote 'Elbows' after reading Lucille Clifton's wonderful poem 'homage to my hips.'"

SUGGESTED READING

Rebellion: Essays 1980–1991 (Firebrand Books)

S/HE (short stories; Firebrand Books)

Walking Back up Depot Street: Poems (University of Pittsburgh Press)

A. K. RAMANUJAN (1929–1993) was born into a Tamil family living in Kannada-speaking Mysore, India. At the time of his death, he was the William E. Colvin Professor at the University of Chicago. Although "A Hindu to His Body" appeared in his first book of poems, *The Striders* (1966), it is evident even in this early piece that Ramanujan is a metaphysical poet: He grapples with the interconnectedness of life, death, and the body. His exploration of the relation between the physical self and the metaphysical self reached its fullest expression in *The Black Hen,* published posthumously in 1995.

SUGGESTED READING

The Collected Poems of A. K. Ramanujan (Oxford University Press)

Folktales from India: A Selection of Oral Tales from Twenty-Two Languages (edited by A. K. Ramanujan; Pantheon Books)

The Man Who Knew Infinity: A Life of the Genius Ramanujan (biography; by Robert Kanigel; Washington Square Press)

The poet RAINER MARIA RILKE (1875–1926) said, "Works of art are indeed always products of having been in danger, of having gone to the very end in an experience, to where man can go no further." He is considered one of the greatest lyric poets of modern Germany. Rilke created the "object poem," attempting to most clearly describe physical objects, the "silence of their concentrated reality."

Rilke's childhood wasn't happy; his parents weren't happily married. They sent him to a military school, hoping he'd become an officer, which he was not inclined to do. Luckily an uncle, who realized Rilke was a gifted young man, helped him to leave the military school and enter a German preparatory school. Rilke studied at the universities of Prague, Munich, and Berlin. His first book of poems was published when he was 19. Rilke traveled throughout his life: to France, Russia, Italy, Spain, and Egypt. He loved Paris and lived there until he was forced to leave during World War I. He spent the war years in Munich and in 1919 went to Switzerland, where he lived for the rest of his life. There he wrote his last two books, *Duino Elegies* and *Sonnets to Orpheus*, both of which brought his work the attention it deserved. His reputation has continued to grow since his death.

SUGGESTED READING

Letters to a Young Poet (nonfiction; translated by Stephen Mitchell; Random House)

Rilke on Love and Other Difficulties: Translations and Considerations of Rainer Maria Rilke (nonfiction; translated by John J. L. Mood; W. W. Norton)

Selected Poems by Rainer Maria Rilke: A Translation from the German and Commentary (translated by Robert Bly; HarperCollins)

RUTH L. SCHWARTZ's (b. 1962) first collection of poems, *Accordion Breathing and Dancing*, won the 1994 Associated Writing Programs Competition. Her second book, *Singular Bodies*, won the 2000 Anhinga Prize for poetry. Schwartz is the recipient of grants from the National Endowment for the Arts, the Astraea Foundation, and the Ohio Arts Council. After working as an AIDS educator for many years, Schwartz now teaches poetry writing at California State University, Fresno.

Schwartz says, "I wrote 'Possible' about a woman I used to see at my neighborhood public swimming pool, but I realized after writing it that it was also an 'ars poetica' of sorts—that is, a poem which reflects the larger vision at work in much of my poetry. I've always been drawn to examine concepts like ugliness and beauty, perfection and damage; and it seems to me that when I observe and write closely about both the body and the natural world, these distinctions break down, are shown to be false, are shown to interpenetrate each other in the kind of complex relationship which is ultimately, I think, what poetry is made of. Most of my poetry deals with the body because I've experienced much joy, and most grief, through my body—and joy and grief, and their intermingling and co-creation, are what largely fuel my work."

SUGGESTED READING

Accordion Breathing and Dancing (poems; University of Pittsburgh Press)

Singular Bodies (poems; Anhinga Press)

WILLIAM SHAKESPEARE (1564–1616) is the world's most famous and respected playwright. He was born in England to middle-class parents, the third child and first son of eight children. His father worked with leather goods and was a dealer in agricultural commodities—a man on the rise, eventually serving as a member of the town council. Shakespeare was probably educated at the King Edward IV Grammar School in Stratford, where he learned Latin and a little Greek and read the Roman dramatists. At 18, he married Anne Hathaway, a woman seven or eight years his senior. Shakespeare wrote more than 30 plays. They were performed in the Globe theater, the most famous playhouse of its time, where people of all different classes would come and sit on different levels of the theater. Only 18 of Shakespeare's plays were published during his lifetime; a complete collection of his works did not appear until the publication of the First Folio in 1623, several years after his death. Nonetheless, his contemporaries recognized Shakespeare's achievements. Shakespeare was a master at creating plays that could be understood and appreciated on multiple levels. Shakespeare's sonnets were written between 1593 and 1601, but not published until 1609. His book, *The Sonnets of William Shakespeare,* consisted of 154 poems, each written in three quatrains and a final couplet, the style of which is now recognized as the Shakespearean form of the sonnet.

SUGGESTED READING

The Complete Poems of Shakespeare (Random House)
The Complete Works of William Shakespeare (Library of Congress Classic)

DEEMA K. SHEHABI (b. 1970) is a writer, editor, and poet. She grew up in the Middle East and attended college in the United States, where she received an M.A. in journalism. Her poems have appeared in several anthologies and literary journals, including *The Poetry of Arab Women* and *The Atlanta Review*. She lives in northern California with her husband, Omar, and son, Fuad-Leith.

About her poem "Breath," she says, "The poem was born out of a deep-rooted desire to link life's outer experiences with the knowledge of life that exists in the body and flows through the veins. In particular, I wanted to explore and describe feelings of fullness and emptiness, happiness and sorrow, and love and loss, as they are reflected in nature, in the faces of my loved ones, and in the universe as a whole. At the end, the poem is a tribute to finding the threads or the gifts that bind us, despite the difficulties, to this earth."

SUGGESTED READING

Shehabi's poems appear in:
The Poetry of Arab Women: A Contemporary Anthology (edited by Nathalie Handal; Interlink Publishing Group)

SIR PHILIP SIDNEY (1554–1586) was an English poet, courtier, and soldier. During his life, he was considered the ideal Renaissance gentleman. His devotion to poetry served as an inspiration for the future writers of English verse. He was educated at Christ Church College in Oxford. A court poet, and a favorite of Elizabeth I, he left the court for a time after falling out of her favor. In 1585 Sidney was appointed governor of Vlissingen in the Netherlands, and in 1586 he joined an expedition to aid the Netherlands against Spain. He died of wounds received during a raid on a Spanish convoy.

None of his work was published during his lifetime. His best-known poems are *Arcadia*, a verse pastoral romance linked by prose passages, and *Astrophel and Stella*, a sequence of 108 sonnets about a hopeless love affair. Sidney's "Defence of Poesie" was an essay describing the nature of poetry and defending it against Puritan objections to imaginative literature. Sidney gives writers good advice with these words, "Fool! said my muse to me, look into thy heart, and write."

SUGGESTED READING

The Making of Sir Philip Sidney (biography; by Edward Berry; University of Toronto Press)

Sir Philip Sidney (selections from his writings; Oxford University Press)

SHEL SILVERSTEIN (1932–1999) was born in Chicago, Illinois, and began writing when he was a young boy. He was a composer, an artist, and the author of many books of prose and poetry for young readers. His books include such modern classics as *The Giving Tree* and *The Missing Piece Meets the Big O*. He's best known for his poetry, much of which is known by heart by many children and adults. Favorite collections include *Where the Sidewalk Ends* and *A Light in the Attic*. Silverstein's work, which he illustrated himself, blends the sly with the serious and the very silly. Silverstein said, "I was so lucky that I didn't have anyone to copy, be impressed by. I had developed my own style; I was creating before I knew there was a Thurber, a Benchley, a Price, and a Steinberg. I never saw their work until I was around 30."

SUGGESTED READING

The Giving Tree (fiction; HarperCollins)
A Light in the Attic (poems; HarperCollins)
The Missing Piece Meets the Big O (fiction; HarperCollins)
Where the Sidewalk Ends (poems; HarperCollins)

PATRICIA SMITH (b. 1955), a popular performance poet, is the undefeated champion of Chicago's nationally famous Uptown Poetry Slam and frequently appears at such poetry venues as New York City's Nuyorican Poets Cafe. Her poems have appeared in *The Paris Review, TriQuarterly, The Nation,* and *Agni.* She grew up in Chicago but now lives in upstate New York, and she is a columnist for *Ms.* magazine.

About the book in which Smith's poem "Skinhead" originally appeared, she says, "[T]he poems beg to be read aloud. If I could visit everyone to read them personally, I would."

SUGGESTED READING

Big Towns, Big Talk (poems; Zoland Books)
Close to Death (poems; Zoland Books)

GARY SOTO (b. 1952) is the author of books for young people as well as for adults. He divides his time between Berkeley and his hometown of Fresno, California.

"In my poem 'Black Hair,' I'm witness to a genius of the baseball diamond named Hector Moreno, a made-up figure who represents every kid athlete who could hit and field five times better than me. As a boy, I was always game to play sports—basketball, football, and, as in the poem, baseball. But I realized my talent was meager and that others could do it spectacularly well. Thus, as a nonplayer of organized sports, I sit in the bleachers. There I cheer for someone who could be me."

SUGGESTED READING

Baseball in April and Other Stories (young adults; Harcourt Brace)

A Summer's Life (short essays, young adults; Laurel Leaf)

Living up the Street: Narrative Recollections (young adults; Laurel Leaf)

Gary Soto: New and Selected Poems (Chronicle Books)

WILLIAM STAFFORD (1914–1993) was born in Kansas. He received a B.A. and an M.A. from the University of Kansas and, in 1954, a Ph.D. from the University of Iowa. During World War II, Stafford was a conscientious objector. He married Dorothy Frantz and they had four children. In 1948 they moved to Oregon, and Stafford took a position at Lewis and Clark College, where he taught until his retirement in 1980. His first major collection of poems, *Traveling Through the Dark*, was published when Stafford was 48. It won the National Book Award in 1963. He went on to publish more than 65 books of poetry and prose. Among his many honors and awards were a Shelley Memorial Award, a Guggenheim Fellowship, and a Western States Lifetime Achievement Award in poetry. In 1970, he was the Consultant in Poetry to the Library of Congress (a position now known as the Poet Laureate). James Dickey noted that Stafford's "natural mode of speech [was] a gentle, mystical, half-mocking and highly personal daydreaming about the western United States." Stafford wrote daily. A story goes that he'd wake early, make himself a cup of instant coffee and a piece of toast, and sit on the living-room couch to write. His method was to take whatever struck his imagination and use that as the inspiration for a poem.

SUGGESTED READING

Even in Quiet Places (poems; Confluence Press)

The Darkness Around Us Is Deep: Selected Poems of William Stafford (edited by Robert Bly; HarperPerennial)
Writing the Australian Crawl: Views on the Writer's Vocation (nonfiction; University of Michigan Press)

MAY SWENSON (1919–1989) is the author of many books of poems. She was born in Utah and received her B.A. from Utah State University. She taught poetry at several universities and was an editor for New Directions Publishers. From 1980 to 1989 she served as a chancellor of the Academy of American Poets. Her work is noted for its elaborate wordplay and surprising use of typography. Her poetry has been been compared to the work of Emily Dickinson and George Herbert.

SUGGESTED READING
Made with Words (essays; Poets on Poetry, University of Michigan Press)
The Love Poems of May Swenson (Houghton Mifflin)
Nature: Poems Old and New (Houghton Mifflin)

The work of poet and writer MARIAHADESSA EKERE TALLIE (b. 1973) has been published in journals in the United States, France, and South Africa, including *Paris/Atlantic, Drumvoices Revue, Long Shot,* and *Carapace.* She is one of nine poets included in the anthology *Listen Up!* Tallie is a senior writer with *African Voices* magazine.

About her poem "Height," Tallie says that she wrote the poem after visiting a Japanese garden. "When the tour guide talked about the bamboo, he emphasized that it is amazingly strong, although it doesn't necessarily look like it is. I thought it was a perfect metaphor for me. I'm a tiny woman who has been through a lot and I'm alive and I'm happy!"

SUGGESTED READING

Tallie's work appears in the following anthologies:

Listen Up!: Spoken Word Poetry (anthology; edited by Zoë Anglesey; One World/Ballantine)

Lest We Forget (Drum FM; CD recording)

NATASHA TRETHEWEY (b. 1966) was born in Mississippi. She has received fellowships from the Alabama State Council on the Arts and the National Endowment for the Arts. Her poems have appeared in many anthologies and magazines, including *Best American Poetry 2000,* the *American Poetry Review,* and the *Gettysburg Review.* Her first book, *Domestic Work,* from which the poems in this anthology are taken, won the 1999 Cave Canem Poetry Prize. Trethewey is currently an assistant professor of creative writing at Emory University.

Speaking about one of her two poems included here, Trethewey says, "When I was writing 'Hot Combs,' I was trying to reckon with having lost my mother, and the knowledge I now had of her suffering over many years prior to her death. I was not ready to confront any of this directly, and so the poem became a way to focus on the body's suffering indirectly—through the act of hair-straightening—and to get closer to an emotional truth. I was struck by the way, as in the depression-era photographs of Dorothea Lange, someone could be made beautiful by physical suffering."

SUGGESTED READING

Domestic Work (poems; Graywolf Press)

Bellocq's Ophelia (poems; Graywolf Press)

DEBORAH TURNER (b. 1968) asks, "What moves and inspires you to breathe from deep down within your chest? Lengthen your throat? Uncurl your shoulders? And allow your inner beauty to radiate out?" For Turner, it can be as simple, as self-indulgently luxurious, as taking a shower. Turner grew up in both the South, mainly Georgia, and in the greater Los Angeles area. She is now a writer and librarian living in Santa Cruz, California.

VAN HANH (d. 1018) descended from a very old family of Vietnamese Buddhists, and was known since childhood for his intelligence. A fervent practitioner of Buddhism, the monk Van Hanh was considered a major prophet. Seen as one of the greatest Vietnamese Buddhist figures, he believed that the true source of Buddhism does not lie in Buddhist writings but through the awakening of each person. Van Hanh was not only a religious man and poet but a patriot as well, involving himself in the defense of national sovereignty. He played a role in the plot to overthrow the dictator King Le Long Dinh.

SUGGESTED READING
A Thousand Years of Vietnamese Poetry (translated by N. Ngoc Bich with others; Knopf)

Poet, novelist, and essayist **ALICE WALKER** (b. 1944) was born in Georgia, the last of eight children. Her parents were sharecroppers; her father earned only $300 a year. She began school at age four and, because of her precociousness, was advanced to first grade. When Walker was eight years old, she lost the sight in one eye when one of her brothers accidentally shot her with a BB gun. She was ostracized by peers because of her scar and turned to reading and writing poetry. Walker was valedictorian of her high-school class and prom queen, and went to college at Spelman, transferring after two years to Sarah Lawrence College in New York. She received her B.A. in 1965. Her daughter, Rebecca, was born in 1969. Walker was an active participant in the civil rights movement in the 1960s, and she continues to be an activist, lending her support to the women's movement, the anti-apartheid movement, the antinuclear movement, and the campaign against female-genital mutilation. Her book *The Color Purple* won her the Pulitzer Prize for fiction in 1983, making Walker the first African-American woman to win this prize. Her other awards include the Lillian Smith Award from the National Endowment for the Arts, a Radcliffe Institute Fellowship, and a Guggenheim Fellowship. She lives in Northern California.

Walker, who wears her hair in dreadlocks, says that Bob Marley was the first person to teach her to "trust the Universe enough to respect her hair." In her book *Living by the Word,* in her essay "Oppressed Hair Puts a Ceiling on the Soul," she says that she saw her hair as the last barrier in her quest for spiritual liberation.

SUGGESTED READING

Anything We Love Can Be Saved: A Writer's Activism (nonfiction; Ballantine)
The Color Purple (novel; Pocket Books)
The Way Forward Is with a Broken Heart (novel; Random House)

WALT WHITMAN (1819–1892) lived in Brooklyn and Long Island in the 1820s and 1830s. At the age of 12, Whitman began to learn the printer's trade. He was largely self-taught and read voraciously. Whitman worked as a printer in New York City until a devastating fire in the printing district demolished the industry. In 1836, at the age of 17, he taught in the one-room schoolhouses of Long Island. In 1841 he turned to journalism full-time and founded a weekly newspaper, the *Long-Islander.* In 1848 Whitman became editor of a New Orleans newspaper. It was in the slave markets of

New Orleans that he witnessed firsthand the viciousness of slavery. When he returned to Brooklyn in 1848, he founded a "free soil" newspaper.

In 1855 Whitman self-published his book *Leaves of Grass*, which consisted of 12 untitled poems and a preface. The book is considered one of the world's major literary works. Whitman's poetry was revolutionary in its time; he liberated poetry—his free verse and rhythmic innovations were starkly different from the poetry of the era, which was marked by strict rhyme schemes and structural patterns.

During his career, Whitman continued to refine the volume, publishing several more editions. Through most of his life, Whitman struggled to support himself. The 1882 publication of *Leaves of Grass* gave Whitman enough money to buy a home. In his simple house, he spent his last years working on additions and revisions to a new edition of the book and preparing his final volume of poems and prose, *Good-Bye, My Fancy*. In "Song of the Open Road," Whitman wrote, "Henceforth I ask not good-fortune . . . ; / Henceforth I whimper no more, postpone no more, need nothing, / Strong and content, I travel the open road."

SUGGESTED READING

Walt Whitman: The Complete Poems (edited by Francis Murphy; Viking Press)

Walt Whitman's America: A Cultural Biography (by David S. Reynolds; Vintage Books)

MILLER WILLIAMS (b. 1930) is the author, editor, or translator of 30 books, including 14 volumes of poetry. Recognition for his work has included the Amy Lowell Travelling Scholarship in poetry from Harvard University. He was the inaugural poet for the second presidential inauguration of Bill Clinton.

Williams took his academic degrees in the sciences after a college counselor, during his freshman year, told him that according to the school's entrance tests, Williams had no verbal aptitude and that if he didn't want to embarrass his parents, he should change his major from English to one of the hard sciences. He taught biological science on the college level for a dozen years, but on the basis of his literary publications, he was offered a position in the English department at Louisiana State University. He is presently University Professor of English and Foreign Languages at the University of Arkansas. He's the father of two-time Grammy Award–winning singer and songwriter Lucinda Williams.

Williams says, "The poem documents an actual dramatic moment in the lives of my family, my friends, and myself when we confronted AIDS for the first time, in the death of one of us."

SUGGESTED READING

Miller Williams and the Poetry of the Particular (essays; edited by Michael Burns; University of Missouri Press)
Some Jazz a While: The Collected Poems (University of Illinois Press)

VIRGINIA WOOLF (1882–1941) is considered the most important and influential woman writer in English of the early twentieth century, credited with innovative novels and bold essays that transformed the way narrative is structured and literature criticized.

She was born in London and educated at home by her parents and by governesses. When she was 13, her mother died, causing her to have a mental breakdown. Woolf was part of an intellectual set who called themselves the Bloomsbury Group (after the area of London in which they lived). She married Leonard Woolf, an important political theorist and socialist, in 1912. She and her husband bought a letter-press and taught themselves typesetting. They started a publishing company in 1917 called The Hogarth Press, which became an important outlet for many contemporary writers, including E. M. Forster and Katherine Mansfield.

Woolf's first novel, *The Voyage Out*, was published in 1915. Her book-length essay *A Room of One's Own*, published in 1929 and regarded as a classic by the feminist movement, was a seminal work in which Woolf said that in order for women to write, they must have the time and space to do so. Woolf wrote, "I would venture to guess that Anon, who wrote so many poems without signing them, was often a woman."

SUGGESTED READING

Moments of Being (excerpts from Woolf's diaries; Harvest Books)

Mrs. Dalloway (novel; Harvest Books)

Orlando (novel; Harvest Books)

A Room of One's Own (nonfiction; Harvest Books)

To the Lighthouse (novel; Harvest Books)

GARY YOUNG (b. 1951) is a poet and artist whose honors include grants from the National Endowment for the Arts, the National Endowment for the Humanities, and the California Arts Council. He has received a Pushcart Prize and the Peregrine Smith Poetry Prize. Forthcoming is a trilogy that includes two previously published books and a new collection titled *If He Had*, due out in the spring of 2002 from Creative Arts Books. He is the coeditor of *The Geography of Home: California's Poetry of Place*. Since 1975 he has designed, illustrated, and printed limited-edition books and broadsides at his Greenhouse Review Press. His print work is represented in numerous collections, including the Museum of Modern Art, and the Victoria and Albert Museum. He lives with his wife and sons in the mountains north of Santa Cruz, California.

About his poem, Young says, "Am I my body? Or is my body a corrupt vessel that serves only to bear my essence, my authentic self? The answer to both of these questions, of course, is yes. We are simultaneously animal bodies that eat, sleep, procreate, and pass away; and spiritual creatures animated by a spark of divine light. Viewing a corpse intensifies the paradox. This is not my father, or my lover, we may say; this is merely an empty husk. But we can look past the slack jaw and the jaundiced skin: We remember when those cold arms once held us. A corpse reveals the pure generosity of being. There is something eternal in all creation. Nothing dies."

SUGGESTED READING

Days (poems; Silverfish Review Press)
The Dream of a Moral Life (poems; Copper Beech Press)
Braver Deeds (poems; Gibbs Smith Publisher)

Permissions

Index of Authors

Index of Titles